SPIRITUAL JOURNEYS

SPIRITUAL JOURNEYS

An anthology of writings by people living and working with those on the margins

Edited by Stanislaus Kennedy RSC

VERITAS

First published 1997 by
Veritas Publications
7-8 Lower Abbey Street
Dublin 1

Copyright © The individual contributors 1997

ISBN I 85390 302 7

British Library Cataloguing
in Publication Data.
A catalogue record for
this book is available
from the British Library.

Cover illustration: 'Crossroads' (oil on canvas, 42 x 45 inches) by
William Crozier. Reproduced by kind permission of the artist.

Cover design by Bill Bolger
Printed in the Republic of Ireland by Betaprint Ltd, Dublin

CONTENTS

FOREWORD

I sense that a new spirituality is being born in the Church today, flowing from the wounded hearts of the weak and broken who are crying out for friendship. This friendship is also a source of healing for those who answer their cry.

Today's world is characterised by the ever-widening gap between the rich and the poor, between the so-called able and the disabled. This gap is not just between Europe and Africa, or between eastern and western Europe. It is within every one of our countries and cities. You just have to take the underground in Paris or walk the streets of any of the big cities to become aware of the growing number of homeless, broken people. The faltering economies of all our societies are engendering new forms of poverty, which create fear in the hearts of the rich who are called to share. We discover then the ever-widening gap between the 'capable', 'admirable' person in each one of us and the broken, weak person also in us.

Jesus came to announce good news to the poor and the lowly. The good news implies that people in community are trying to bridge this terrible gap. But this is not easy. It means that the broken and the lowly come out from behind their walls of despair and dare to believe and trust in themselves and in others. It means also that the rich and the comfortable allow themselves to be dispossessed and to start walking on the road of insecurity. Bridging the gap is not just giving food and lodging to those who are hungry and homeless and praying for them. It means eating with them, living with them, praying with them. Isn't this Jesus' vision when he invites us to eat with the poor, the disabled and the blind (see Luke 14)? If we do so, then we will be blessed, says Jesus. This blessedness is the amazing discovery that living in communion with the lowly becomes a source of healing. To be healed by the poor is at the heart of the Gospel message. Then we discover that Jesus is hidden in the poor.

This book, edited by Sister Stan, is about bridging the gap and about being healed by the poor and the lowly. It is a book of hope.

Jean Vanier

PREFACE

Bringing this book into being was no easy task. Neither was it easy to write my own contribution to it. It came about because for many years several people, including and especially Jean Vanier, had suggested that I should write the story of my own spiritual journey. It was an invitation I resisted strongly, mainly because it was much easier for me to write about issues than to write about myself. To write about myself, I felt, would be to reveal who I am – in so far as I know it – to all who choose to read it, and this did not come easily to me.

There was also another reason why I found it hard to write about my own spiritual journey, and that had to do with a feeling that in writing I might be perceived as claiming that I am different from others, or that I have done more than others who haven't written about themselves, and I know in my heart that that is not the case. I am aware that I often acted from mixed motives, and furthermore, I know that whatever my life's work has been about, it was helped and enhanced by many people who came into my life.

So why then did I decide to go ahead and write my own story after all? What happened was that another person, who has also written in this book, came and told me their story one day, and I found myself saying to them, You must write this down. I was asking somebody to do what I had resisted doing myself. That led me to reflect on the invitation more, and as I prayed through it, I became more and more aware that all was gift, that all I was, had and did was a graced gift from God to me. And all I was asked to do was to express that gift and give thanks for it. This meant having the humility to name and claim and share that gift, and sharing was not only sharing in the service of the poor, but also speaking and writing about it as honestly as was possible for me, without a tinge of boastfulness, because it wasn't mine, but only what was given to me in trust.

This led me to the idea of inviting others to do the same, so I wrote to people I knew (I know all the contributors personally except one) and invited them to write about their internal and external journeys as part of a collection of essays. Most of them said they found it difficult to do, but having reflected on it, they all agreed, and they not only agreed, but they submitted their essays to me exactly within the time frame we had fixed.

This is a book about the individual spiritual journeys of people with a Christian commitment to working with God's marginalised people – the poor, the dying, people with physical or learning disabilities, the homeless, prostitutes – in various parts of the world. But though the authors are scattered over the world, in Canada, the United States, Europe, Britain and Ireland, we all share a common belief in the value of working with the people society rejects, and we have many experiences in common.

All the people who have contributed to this book have felt ourselves called in a special way to the work we do. Many of us have pursued other paths at other times in our lives. We had no plans to do the work we have found ourselves doing. For us, God's way was unknown and unplanned, but nevertheless we felt ourselves drawn into this work. God broke through in our lives.

A theme that runs through all these writings is how we are all taught by those we serve. These little people, the rejected ones, the abandoned ones, these fragile people who are without wealth or possessions, without homes, without employment, often without even families and ordinary human love, these are the ones who became teachers of us, the people who have the privilege of working with them and serving them in their daily lives. Many of the authors are seen as modern prophets, and indeed that is what they are – people who read the signs of the times in the light of the Gospel that the world may be transformed. But the people we work with – people experiencing poverty, exclusion and powerlessness in many different parts of the world – these people too are prophets and teachers. These are the people who shout at us about our selfishness, our greed and our materialism. It is through daily contact with these unexpected prophets that the authors of these essays have come to learn about the beauty and dignity of the human person and the value of love.

Not that the people we live and work with are all sweetness and light. Far from it. They are often angry and violent. But anger and violence are masks worn by lonely and frightened and rejected people. It is our task as people who work with marginalised and rejected people to see the beauty of the human beings behind those masks, and to reveal that beauty to the world.

The people whose writings you are holding in your hand are people who come into daily contact with pain. The agony of the world is written in the human faces we meet every day. But we also come into daily contact with hope, in the fragile people we work with, in people who start each day afresh, in people who are sick, have disabilities, are out of work, out of home, in people who, in spite of terrible experiences, are able to be strong and to be a source of hope to others.

Hope is what we are called to as Christians. It is no trivial task to give an account of the hope that is in us in the midst of overwhelming poverty, in the face of sickness, through grief and derision and loneliness, speaking forcefully and without malice, restructuring our priorities and making credible our value systems, plodding patiently through daily tasks and commitment. The call to release life and meaning from all the secret and dim events of our personal and communal histories is our challenge as Christians. We are called to probe the forbidden, to unmask monsters, to look death in the eye; we are called to love in love's inimitable way by service and sacrifice. Hope lives on the edge, between the near and the far, the future and the infinite, the now and the not yet. Our spirits may be weak, our bodies tired, but we hunger still for good news, and in that lies our hope.

For Christians, Noah's Ark is the ultimate symbol of hope, that brave and fragile vessel with its human and animal cargo, tossed on the swollen waters of the world and finally lodging on a mountaintop as the waters recede. And it is no coincidence that Jean Vanier's L'Arche is a central and powerful source of inspiration for so many of the writers in this book. Long and safely may it sail on the waters of adversity.

Finally, I would like to thank all the contributors to the book and their publishers for their co-operation; also William Crozier who gave his kind permission to reproduce the painting on the cover; and Siobhán Parkinson for help with copy-editing and proofing.

Stanislaus Kennedy RSC

UNDERSTANDING OUR OWN BROKENNESS: THE PATH TO HEALING

Jean Vanier

We live in a very broken world. What we have seen happening in Rwanda and in Bosnia shows us something of the pain and anger in the world. Such events often seem quite distant and remote from our day-to-day lives, but I believe they are symptomatic of the pain and anger that we can feel within ourselves.

Over the past thirty years I have had the joy of welcoming a number of men and women from psychiatric institutions to L'Arche. When these people with mental handicaps arrived in the community they often had a lot of anger and depression inside them. I have seen them gradually change. I could even say that I have often been a witness to a kind of resurrection in them which is a source of hope for me. I would like to tell you a bit of what I have learned from these people. I believe that by understanding their brokenness, we can understand more of our own brokenness; and that by opening ourselves up and being willing to relate to others, we can be healed. In this way we can enter into forgiveness and reconciliation between people in a small but fundamental way.

Luisito

We welcomed Luisito into our community in Santo Domingo in the Dominican Republic. Luisito used to be a beggar in the street. He is a man with severe disabilities; he is unable to walk or talk, or eat by himself. His mother would sit close to him as he lay on the streets and people gave them money. When his mother died, Luisito was left all alone. A group of people in the local parish found a little shack for him and took turns looking after him. Each day someone would feed and bathe him. This same group asked L'Arche to open a community in Santo Domingo. After some time, we set up a community there and the first person we welcomed was Luisito.

Luisito was full of anger and depression. He did not want to live. We wanted him to live, though. We had meals with him, all together at the table. We tried to encourage him to walk and to work. We wanted him to grow, but that was our desire, not his. In our communities, the force of hope of the assistants often has to be stronger than the force of despair of people like Luisito.

Luisito has begun to walk and even though he grumbles a bit, he has started to work. Life is beginning to flow in him; he wants to live. That does not mean, of course, that all the anger and depression are gone. They are still there and can come to the surface again, but healing is taking place. It is beautiful to see the gradual transformation in this man.

We in L'Arche do not expect Luisito to be suddenly healed and to suddenly walk and talk. That is not the kind of healing we experience in our communities. Healing in L'Arche is a gradual acceptance of self, a discovery of our own beauty in spite of our brokenness. It is the discovery that no matter how deeply wounded we may be, there is beauty inside us. It is about discovering the desire to live. It took me a long time to realise this.

The story of L'Arche

I joined the navy when I was thirteen and left eight years later. In the navy, I was part of a very competitive world, where we were taught to be efficient, to be quick, to win, to sink the enemy's ships before we ourselves were sunk. It is a world with a few winners and many losers. In 1950 I left the navy to follow Jesus and to learn more about the good news of the Gospels. In 1963, my friend Father Thomas Philippe OP invited me to meet some of his new friends: thirty men with a mental handicap living in a small institution in northern France. My friend had discovered the truth of Paul's words in his letter to the Corinthians where he writes that God chose the foolish in this world to confound the wise; the weak of the world, to confound the strong (1 Co 1:27). My friend had seen how the men he was living with were carriers of good news. They had suffered rejection and hurt, and he was discovering something in their simplicity and freedom.

I came to visit them. I was embarrassed, not knowing quite how to communicate with people who couldn't talk very well, and wondering, even if they could, what we would talk about. But I was touched by these men. By some word or gesture or through the look in their eyes they seemed to be saying to me, 'Do you love me?' At the time, I was teaching philosophy at the University of Toronto where my students were interested in my intelligence, in what I could teach them, so that they could pass their exams. But these men didn't care about what was in my head; they were interested in my person, in my heart and in my capacity to relate.

These men asked another question, verbally or non-verbally: 'Why? Why am I like this? Why have my parents put me into this institution? Why do I fall on the ground? Why can't I be like my brothers and sisters and get married?' That was my introduction to the world of losers.

I began to visit psychiatric institutions of all sorts where I discovered an immense world of people in pain. Thousands of people with psychiatric disorders or learning disabilities had been shut up in institutions for the rest of their lives. It shocked me. I had come from a world of winners, people who succeed. I had had little contact with the world of the losers. I became aware of all the barriers that had existed between my way of life and the life of many other people. It shocked me to realise that for thirty years I had been totally ignorant of so much pain and brokenness in the world.

Visiting one institution, I met Raphael Simi. He had had meningitis when he was a child and had lost the capacity to speak and to walk with ease. I also met Philippe Seux who had a similar story: he had had encephalitis, as a result of which one leg and one arm were paralysed. Philippe was able to speak. In fact, he spoke too much, lived in a world of dreams. When their parents had died, Raphael and Philippe were put into an institution without being consulted. It was an institution for about eighty men in two dormitories of forty. They had no work, nothing to do all day. I invited Raphael and Philippe to come and live with me in a small house I had purchased with the help of friends. I obtained the necessary permission from local authorities and we began to live together. I did the cooking, so we ate very badly. I knew something about warships and about Aristotle, but nothing about people with handicaps.

Living together, we began to know each other. As I listened to them, I began to discover their beauty, their simplicity, but also their pain; what it means for a man or a woman to sense all their lives that they are a disappointment. I had parents who loved, trusted and supported me; they listened to me. These two men had lived a completely opposite reality. I can understand the terrible pain and disappointment of parents when their child is born with a handicap. They were expecting a beautiful, healthy child, but they realise that their child is sick and that this sickness will have vast consequences. Perhaps the child will never be able to talk. Yes, the pain of parents is immense, but children also suffer pain, especially the pain of rejection. Raphael and Philippe had experienced great pain. They had anger in them and suffered from a broken self-image.

I was also beginning to realise that they weren't particularly keen to live with an ex-naval officer who thought he could tell everybody what to do. Nor did they want to live with an ex-philosophy teacher who thought he knew everything. What they wanted was a friend, somebody who would love and accept them just as they were, who would not reject them when he discovered their limits, their brokenness, and their vulnerability. They needed someone who saw their potential, who wanted to help them to grow and to do something beautiful with their lives. They needed a friend who was happy that they existed and who wanted to be with them. Living together, eating around the same table each day, I began to see more clearly the meaning of Jesus' words:

> When you give a meal do not invite your family, your rich neighbours, your friends, because when you invite them you probably want to be invited in return.

> Instead, when you give a banquet invite the poor, the lame, the crippled, the blind, and then you will be blessed.
> (Luke 14)

As I grow older, I appreciate Jesus more and more and I discover his incredible vision of humanity. I think I can say that at L'Arche I have experienced that blessedness of eating at the table of the poor.

It was quite obvious that Raphael and Philippe needed me. It was not so obvious, however, how much I needed them. In some mysterious way, they were healing me, helping me to become more whole. Maybe that is what healing is about, becoming whole, discovering who we are, and discovering all the powers of tenderness as well as the powers of violence in us. To discover our beauty and our brokenness, and to realise that through all that, we can grow in love; we can love each other. We can become a people of hope.

Other people came to help in L'Arche and so we began to eat a bit better! We welcomed more people from institutions. The original community has grown and now we have more than a hundred communities in various parts of the world.

Antonio

About six years ago we welcomed Antonio. He is a very fragile man who cannot walk or talk or use his arms. He is under constant oxygen and dependent on others in every way. He lives in one of our homes with five people like him and five others who have the privilege of living with and caring for them. If you visit that home and come close to Antonio and call him by his name, his face breaks out into a smile, his eyes light up. He is an incredibly beautiful man. He shows no depression, no signs of revolt. He seems to totally accept who he is, and his beauty flows from his eyes and from his whole being. He has a capacity to love that many of us have lost. We may have a capacity to be generous, to do things for people, and that is good. But often we do not know how to receive from others. Antonio cannot be generous, but he can love simply, with trust. Through his face, his eyes, his gestures, his whole body, he says: 'I love you and I trust you.' That's an amazing gift! Trust is a gift of our heart and of our intelligence to another. To trust is something very beautiful but often we do not know how to trust people. In losing trust we try to prove ourselves. Antonio can't prove anything. He does not ask for money or for knowledge or for power. He just asks: 'Do you love me? Do you want to enter into a relationship with me?'

If you talk with the assistants who live with Antonio many will tell you that he has transformed their lives. They come from a competitive and aggressive world, where people have to prove themselves. They come from a world where they have to show that they're capable and strong. Antonio has led them into a world of tenderness and of trust. When you give Antonio a bath, when you spend time with him, you have to be at peace with yourself. If you are nervous or angry or in a state of conflict, Antonio feels it through your hands. Antonio asks you to be still inside, he calls you to inner peace and healing, to stillness. He calls you to be very attentive to his fragile little body. He may not be able to speak with words, but he communicates with his whole body. A lot of the people with whom we live cannot speak, but their violence, their depression, their smiles are a language. They speak with their eyes, face, hands, their no or their yes, with their smile or with their anger. When you live with somebody like Antonio you become sensitive to the expression on people's faces and to the way they use their hands. We often hide our real thoughts behind our words, but our bodies do not lie, they reveal what is really happening inside.

Eric

When I left the leadership of the community, I lived in one of our houses with ten men and women like Antonio. Every morning I would give Eric his bath. Eric has died now, but he was blind, deaf and couldn't walk. As I began to enter into a relationship with him through the bathing, I began to discover how important it was to relate to his body, and in relating to his body, to relate to my own. The meaning of Paul's words became clear to me: 'Do you not know that your body is the temple of the Spirit, that the Spirit of God is living in you' (1 Co 6:19). I became aware of the mystery of the presence of God in this little broken body, and realised that if God is present in Eric, God is also present in me. That changes everything in our relationships.

Helen

I visited our community in the Philippines some time ago. I had time to talk with Keiko, a Japanese assistant, who was often holding Helen in her arms. Keiko said that it was not always easy with Helen. Helen was very fragile; she was blind and could not walk or talk. But what Keiko found so difficult was that Helen had no reaction. She was never angry, she never smiled, she showed no emotion, she was apathetic. We talked about depression and about what happens when a child goes into depression. I suggested that Keiko continue to touch Helen, to talk to her, to sing to her, to be very attentive to her. I told her that maybe one day Helen would smile. And I asked her to send me a postcard if she ever did. Three months later I received a postcard that said: 'Helen smiled at me this morning. Love Keiko'.

Why does a child like Helen go into depression? Why does she hide? Why at some particular moment does she comes out of it? Each one of us spent about nine months in our mother's womb, where the incredible journey of each one of our lives began. From the moment of our conception, through birth and into adulthood, there is gradual growth, until the time of loss begins. With old age we become once again like the little child we used to be, totally dependent on others. This is our journey, from the littleness of the child to the littleness of the weak, old and dying person. It's an incredible thing when a child is born, so fragile, so weak, unable to do anything by him- or herself. If a baby is hungry she cannot go to the fridge or if she's cold she cannot pull up the blankets. The child is totally vulnerable. That vulnerable child is still in us. If we're loved there's incredible peace. To know that all that is fragile, broken and little is loved is a beautiful experience for the child. To love someone is not to do things for them, it is to reveal to them that they are beautiful, that they have value, that they are unique, precious. That's what a child needs, and that's what the mother, the father, the aunts and uncles, the grandparents reveal to the child: he or she is beautiful. The child doesn't need to prove anything, doesn't have to prove his or her capacities; the child just has to know that he or she is loved.

But what happens if the child is not loved? What happens if the child at one moment begins to sense that he or she is not wanted? That leads to a terrible feeling of loneliness, a painful inner void, a feeling that nobody wants him or her, that nobody loves him or her. This sort of loneliness is anguish, an inner agitation that can break the cycle of sleep as well as the cycle of digestion. From loneliness springs guilt or shame: 'If I'm not loved it means I'm no good, I'm not lovable.'

John
In my community we welcomed a man called John, who was going through a very bad period of hallucinations. We had a meeting with our psychiatrist and all the people who were close to John. The psychiatrist told us that he believed that John felt guilty about existing, that he felt he had always been seen as a

nuisance. His parents didn't want him 'like that'. His grandparents took him for a time after that, but eventually didn't want him either. Then he was placed with a family but he was a nuisance to them too. He ended up in a psychiatric ward, always seen as a nuisance. That is difficult for a child. He is bound to develop the psychology of the victim who thinks: 'Nobody can love me. I'm no good.'

When *we* are lonely, we can do things to forget the loneliness and the inner pain. We can ring somebody up. We can watch television or read a book. But what happens when a child is caught up in this world of anguish, inner pain, or guilt for existing? What can a child do to escape from the anguish? The child's response is often to slip into a dream-world in order to run away from and forget the pain. The child may break off all form of communication and sulk and close up. That was Helen's way of dealing with inner pain. Her parents didn't want her 'like that'. They made her feel that she was no good, so she experienced a terrible loneliness, inner pain and feelings of guilt. It's not possible to live with such inner anguish. I remember a young girl telling me that she would rather live in a dream-world than in reality, as reality was too painful for her. She said she felt better when she was in the dream. I told her that I understood that reality can be too difficult to live with where there is not enough love, acceptance, or recognition of who you are. It is easier to escape into a world of dreams and lock yourself up in it. But I told her also that the problem is that in a dream-world you are alone. And I said that I hoped that one day she would have enough inner force to negotiate with reality, to accept reality and to find the friends who would help her to live reality.

That is what had happened to Helen. She had slipped away. She cut herself off from all relationships and went into a world inside herself. Relationships can be very dangerous, because there is always the danger that the other person will withdraw from the relationship and leave you alone. We all have difficulties with relationships. We are frightened that if we give our heart, our secret, to another and then he or she leaves us, or does not want us, then we will be left alone with our anguish and our emptiness. This can make us think it is better not to love, not to relate, but just to do things, to succeed, to be powerful, to be independent, not to need anyone else.

So it was with Helen. She had hidden herself away in her own inner world, locked herself up in the prison of her solitude. She would only come out if somebody could love her with enough unconditional love and say to her 'I love you just as you are. I want to be with you.' All this had to be said through touch, through the way she was carried, through the tone of a voice. At one moment Helen tasted love. She recognised that somebody appreciated her in her littleness and her brokenness. It's an incredible thing for people to experience love and a communion of hearts. And so she dared to open the door of her heart and to come out. She began to smile and then she smiled more. She came out of herself as much as she could.

Lucien

People with disabilities have taught me a lot not only about tenderness but also about other things. Lucien came into our community some years ago. He has severe mental and physical handicaps. He had lived all his life with his mother who had a deep understanding of her son. She understood all his non-verbal language. However, when she became sick and went to hospital, Lucien could not stay alone and was sent to another hospital. So, at the age of thirty, for the first time in his life he lived the experience of broken communion. He fell into a world of anguish and pain. This was the first time that he had been separated from the only person who loved him. Eventually he came to our community, into one of the houses where I was living. When Lucien went into his bouts of anguish he would scream. The pitch of his voice was very high and piercing. It was as if his screams of pain and of anguish entered into me and became my screams of anguish; his cries resonated with my cries as a child, which I had pushed down inside me. He awoke something deep within me: a violence, an anger and an inner pain. I found that very difficult. Fortunately, I had community, brothers and sisters, who helped me to see the anguish and to manage and calm it. I can understand that if people are too alone in front of such anguish they can react with violence.

In the United States it is said that battered children are the most frequent admissions in children's hospitals. My experience with Lucien helped me to understand what can happen to a mother who has been abandoned by her husband, who has a deep lack of affection and who is depressed. She experiences aggression at work and on the way home spends time shopping. When she arrives home, she is completely exhausted. Her children want to touch her and to be hugged and loved by her. They need to communicate with her. The mother can't. Her well of affection is empty. She has no more strength inside her to relate or to communicate with them, to touch and to love them. She herself has too much inner pain. And so she just gives them something to eat, but they don't want food. They want nourishment for their hearts, not just material food. She puts them in front of the television, but they don't want that. They want reality; they want her attention. And so they provoke her, and finally the mother hits one of them and then she breaks into tears.

We all have defence mechanisms, which make us selective. We choose some people and reject others. We are prejudiced against some people; we don't want to get close to them. We know that behind our defence mechanisms is a world of vulnerability. Our defence mechanisms protect us from our own tenderness and our capacity to love and to relate to others. When we live with people with disabilities, our defence mechanisms are shattered or at least weakened. Living with Raphael, Philippe, Antonio and others like them, I discovered that their need is for tenderness, understanding, a certain proximity or the right distance in a relationship.

When our defence mechanisms are lowered or weakened, our

powers of anger and our capacity to hurt others are allowed to emerge. I was shocked to see what was inside me, but it was also a realisation that this is what it is to be human. We can all talk to people, we can all love people, we can all hurt people. We hurt them by active violence or by ignoring them, by not wanting to know about them, by leaving them shut up in institutions and by refusing any form of solidarity with those who are broken. We can choose to remain in our own little world of prejudices. If we become close to some people, they awaken the anger and fear in us. Living with Lucien made me realise that to be fully human means to touch the powers of tenderness, but also the powers of violence within us, the violence and tenderness that are contained behind defence mechanisms that have been built up in us since our childhood. I found it difficult to accept this in myself, but at the same time it was important for me to realise that this is who I am and to be able to talk about it with other people. This has helped me to realise more fully what it means to be human.

At that time, I discovered a letter that Carl Jung had written to a Christian woman in Strasbourg. It touched me very much. Jung wrote to this woman:

> I admire you Christians, because when you see somebody hungry and thirsty you see Jesus, when you visit somebody in prison or sick, you visit Jesus, or when you welcome a stranger or clothe a naked person you are in communication with Jesus. What I do not understand is that you do not see Jesus in your own poverty. Why do you see the poor only outside of yourself? You seem incapable of seeing the poverty inside yourself. You seem to be denying that poverty. Why do you think you have to be better than others and do things for people when you yourself also have a brokenness inside you? Why can't you see Jesus hidden in your own brokenness? Why do you deny it?

That letter was a little light which helped me along the road.

Not so long ago, one of our community leaders in L'Arche told me about his mother. He said that she was quite a young woman but she had Alzheimer's disease. She had become very small and weak; she could not even brush her teeth any more. He also told me that his father had always been quite a powerful man, very capable in industry, organisation and business. He tended to put more into organisation and production than into relationships. When his wife became sick, he didn't want her put in hospital. So he decided to keep her at home and look after her himself. This had transformed him, he said. This highly efficient, capable, powerful man had entered a world of attentiveness, of tenderness, of kindness and of listening. In some mysterious way, this man was being healed by his wife.

René

René was in my community for some time. Like a lot of people, he doesn't like to work. Instead of working he would hitch-hike on the main road. He was well-dressed, so people stopped for him. When a car stopped and the driver opened the window, René would put practically his whole body right through the window, and say, 'Give me a cigarette!' The driver would become quite nervous and do anything to find cigarettes or money to buy cigarettes in order to get this body out of his car. René made more money hitch-hiking than in the workshops, until we helped him to go to another community where the main road was further away.

Once René went for a week's retreat with some of the people of his community. They sang and did mimes and spoke about the Gospels. One day they spoke about a passage from Revelation.

> I stand and I knock at the door. If anyone hears me knocking, opens the door and lets me come in, I will eat with that person and that person will eat with me. (Rv 3:20).

It is a gentle text about Jesus knocking at the door of our innermost consciousness. When René heard it, he said that when Jesus comes to eat with him, he knows exactly what they will eat. Then he gave the whole menu: pancakes and mussels and cider! Then he continued: 'And when he comes, he will tell me something.' When they asked what Jesus would tell him, he answered: 'He will take me in his arms and say, "You are my beloved son."' Is there a more beautiful definition of prayer? It is very simple: he will take me in his arms and say: 'You are my beloved son, my beloved daughter.'

Didier

Didier, who lives in my house, has a special sickness: his body is always in movement. It is not easy for him. After a community weekend I asked him what had touched him the most during the weekend. Didier told me that when the priest was speaking, his heart was burning. If I had asked him what the priest had said, I am sure he would not have been able to tell me. It was the music of the voice that he had heard. For Didier it is not a question of concepts or of language. What is most important for people like Didier, Antonio, Raphael and Philippe is presence, community, the way people come together and the tone of their voices. When people are close to each other, relating one to another, without manipulation, without possessing, then they create a world of celebration.

Jean-Claude

In our communities we are not always terribly serious. Normal people are more serious. They need people to come and give them talks. And when you give them talks, they're all silent. In our community it is not like that. People interrupt you all the time. Normal people are a strange group. They have problems with the Church, problems in their families, problems with money, problems with work, problems in politics. They're often worried and sad. I was talking one day with a man who was very normal. There was a knock on the door and Jean-Claude came in. Some people say that Jean-Claude is mongol, others say that he's Down's syndrome. We just call him Jean-Claude. Jean-Claude laughs a lot. He's very relaxed. He came in and shook hands with Mr Normal and laughed, and then he shook hands with me and laughed, and he went on his way and laughed. Mr Normal looked at me and he said, 'Isn't it sad, people like that?'

The problem with Mr Normal is that he's blinded by his prejudices and fears, and he's unable to see that Jean-Claude is happy. There's no problem with Jean-Claude. There are lots of problems with Mr Normal.

The path of healing

So how can healing come about? In this broken world, where Mr Normal has created a world of prejudice and theory and intellectual stuff and shoved away the Jean-Claudes, how can we bring them together so that we can heal each other? Maybe Jesus is giving the answer to that when he tells us to love our enemies. The Christian message is very powerful. I say to you, love your enemies, do good to those who hate you, speak well of those who speak evil of you, and pray for those who push you down and persecute you. Maybe loving your enemy is somehow to enter into the path of healing, into the whole business of forgiveness and reconciliation.

Maybe when we reject people we are saying something about our own brokenness, our own incapacity to love, and maybe we will be healed by those we reject, and enter into communication with them. Jesus says, Don't try to pick a speck of dust out of someone's eye. Can't you see that you have a log in your own eye? Take out the log so that you can see clearly to take the speck of dust out of the eye of another person. How quickly we are blinded about ourselves! How easily we are frightened of discovering who we are! But maybe as we turn to those whom we reject we will be healed. Maybe that is what we are beginning to discover in L'Arche, that we're on a path of healing together, discovering that we need each other. Those that we reject are revealing something about our own brokenness, and as we put our hand in theirs, then maybe we begin our journey on the path of healing.

HOSPITALITY ON THE MARGINS

Dara Molloy

There are those who are marginalised by outside forces and there are those who choose to live on the margins. I am one of those who has chosen to live on the margins. For this reason, I do not identify myself as someone who works with the marginalised, or even as one who lives with the marginalised, even though that is true also. My identity lies in being on the margins myself.

Geographically, I live on the margins of Europe. My home is on an island off an island off an island off Europe! This island, Inismór, one of the three Aran Islands, is ten miles off the coast and is exposed to the full force of the Atlantic. As an island, it was remote and inaccessible up to about ten years ago. When I came to live here in January 1985, I had to travel to Galway the night before sailing, board a cargo vessel at Galway docks at six o'clock the next morning and endure seven hours on the sea in freezing weather before docking at Inismór around lunchtime. That sailing was only available twice a week, weather permitting, and the only other option was to fly. Since then, tourism has opened up the island, and a ferry from Rossaveel can now take you there in thirty-five minutes.

Apart from the geographical margins, I am also on the margins of society. By choosing to live on an island, in a Gaeltacht (Irish-speaking) area, I have moved in the opposite direction to the mainstream. Islands around Ireland have had a continuous trend of depopulation since the Famine – a trend even more severe than the rest of rural Ireland. Around the time of the Famine (1847) 3,000 people lived on Inismór. Now there are only 750. In the eleven years that I have been on the island, the population has been reduced by 150 from 900.

Detaching myself from the mainstream has also meant

choosing to live simply and to produce my own food and other requirements myself. My income is so low that I don't pay income tax. When I collect a half-dozen eggs from my chickens, I don't have to pay for the carton, nor am I paying for the transportation of the eggs half-way across the country, causing pollution, environmental degradation and burning up of non-renewable fossil fuel. And of course, the eggs taste better! Opting out of the mainstream has meant living on a low income, without a bank mortgage and without a car. However, I experience the way I live as very satisfying and very fulfilling. Living on the margins, for me, has been a good choice.

I also live on the margins of the Church. Until the summer of 1996, I was still a Church member, still a practising priest, and still a member of a religious order, although I had moved to the edge of all these institutions. However, I have now resigned from these organisations also. My priesthood is now the priesthood that Jesus exercised, of the order of Melchizedek (Hb 7:1-28). The authority I claim for exercising it is the same authority that Jesus claimed and that John the Baptist claimed (Mt 21:23-27).

I describe myself as being de-institutionalised and de-professionalised. I do not work directly for any bishop or any religious order. I have no 'job'. I am not a curate or a parish priest, nor am I any longer a schoolteacher. Nobody pays me a wage, not even the State in the form of dole. In this sense, I am a nobody. I cannot be identified by my work.

Unemployed people, of course, are the same. I have plenty of work to do and I work very hard, but I am not working for an employer or for an institution. Nor am I working to make a living, so I cannot say I am self-employed either. I do not work to make money. I work because I see work that needs to be done and I can do it. My work is varied. It includes gardening, work with animals, building, writing, giving talks, offering hospitality, prayer, liturgy, ritual, answering letters, committees, projects, etc. My income comes through this work in various ways and I make enough to live on.

Our society gives identity and status to people according to their work. People with no work are then left without a place in that society. This applies not only to people who are unemployed, but also to retired people, people with handicaps, and people who do work which is not paid or recognised as valuable. In my own life, I have chosen to join these people on the margins in a positive way. I wish to emphasise that my value lies not in the work that I do, as such, but in the person that I am. My works are my fruits, and these fruits may be in an area outside of the employment market or the gross national product. I will not accept economists as my judge and jury. I stand in solidarity with other people who are undervalued by our society.

My hero is John the Baptist. He was a man who chose to live on the margins. He left the towns and villages of Judaea and shook the dust off his feet as he went to live in the desert. The place he chose was along the Jordan river about twenty miles from Jerusalem. Twenty miles in those days was a day's journey on foot. John chose not to wear the clothes that were commonly worn at that time. He wore animal skins. He also preferred not to eat the food of the people of his day. Instead he chose a diet of wild locusts and honey. I like him for this. In a visible and symbolic way, he made a strong statement about the world he was living in. He could not participate in it. My feelings are the same and so I try to imitate John. I normally don't wear clerical or religious clothes, and my food is unpackaged, unprocessed, mostly vegetarian, and organically home-produced. Our new home has been built by ourselves with the help of our friends, without using building contractors. We have used local material where possible and second-hand material where we could get it.

John the Baptist left the mainstream of Jewish society to live in the desert because he did not like the direction that society was taking. In order to maintain his own integrity, he had to detach himself from any collusion with society's false values and errant direction. From a position of strength and independence on the margins of Jewish society, John was able to see more clearly what was going on. Free from being tainted or compromised by it in his own life, he was the better able to speak out against it. John confronted the people of Israel with the picture he saw. His call was for conversion.

I feel a bit like John the Baptist. Standing at my front door I can face east and look out over the coast of Connemara. I am looking out at the whole of Ireland, even the whole of Europe. If I go out my back door and climb the hill a bit, I can look west out over the Atlantic towards America and the rest of the world. From this position, I feel detached and removed from what goes on in the world. I am not uninterested, but living on the island gives me a better perspective. Like John the Baptist, I do not like the direction our western society is taking – consumerism, environmental destruction, breakdown of community, increased violence, loss of spirituality. I don't want to participate in its onward rush towards destruction. In coming to the island, I have freed myself enough to make space for a different way of living, based on different values. In my new way of life, I feel stronger and more secure in the attempts I make to confront the people and institutions of the mainstream with what is happening. I do this by speaking to the groups and individuals who come to visit us. I also do it by publishing a magazine, *The Aisling*. Another of my heroes from the Old Testament is Abram (who became Abraham). Abram was getting on in years, and appeared to be very comfortable where he lived among the rich valleys of the Tigris and Euphrates. Yet, although he was in his seventies, wealthy, married, with large herds of sheep and goats, there was a restlessness within him, a desire to get up and move. Eventually, he responded to that desire and headed off west 'to a place that God would show him'. In this act of blind trust he gave birth to the Jewish faith, and to the Christian and Muslim faiths which followed.

So Abram's great achievement was not some heroic deed or some wonderful creation. It was the simple act of moving out into the unknown, in response to some inner calling. By removing himself from a defined and fixed environment, he left room in his life for the spirit of God to work.

I like Abram for this reason. As St Paul writes in Romans 4, Abram was 'justified' not because he kept the Ten Commandments, was circumcised, or obeyed the Torah. He lived before all of these things came into existence or became requirements. If Abram could be 'justified before God', we can all be 'justified before God'. It does not matter if we are unemployed, penniless, or never passed an exam. All of us will be justified before God if we allow space in our lives for God to act. If we have the courage to follow the call of the spirit within us, then God does act.

Abram's blind act of trust was taken up as an example to be followed by the early Irish monks. Young monks wandered the earth, both in Ireland and across Europe, looking for their 'place of resurrection'. They experienced a leading of the spirit, symbolised as travelling on a boat without sail, oar or rudder. They believed they would be shown by God where they were to settle and build their hermitages. This would be their place of resurrection.

There is a story about St Jarlath. He was told by St Brendan (the Navigator) that he should drive his chariot until the wheel broke. Wherever it broke, there he should build his monastery. Jarlath's chariot wheel broke at Tuam and so he built his monastery there. It is now the seat of the archdiocese of Tuam. The episcopal ring bears an engraving of the broken wheel.

Many young people today set off on a personal search, looking for clues as to what they should do with their lives. Sometimes they travel within their own country, sometimes around the world. They allow some inner intuition to guide them to places far away from home. Often they keep wandering until they find their true home, a person to marry, an occupation to fulfil them, or a place to settle down. What they find becomes for them their place of resurrection, something that will stand to them against the difficulties of life. If people can find some deep meaning for their lives, they will be able to withstand all the hardships that come their way, even death itself. Finding their place of resurrection ensures their victory over the forces of death. Their lives will be fruitful, like Abram's, because they have found and followed their calling.

I too experienced the call of Abram. It came not so much when I felt a calling to become a priest, in my early teens, but much later when I was already ordained and teaching in a school. From an onlooker's perspective I had achieved my goal. I had done well at school, succeeded in university and was now an ordained priest. I had reached a place in society that gave me a high status and a comfortable life. That should have settled me.

But instead of feeling fulfilled and sustained in my role as a priest and religious, I found the opposite. I felt suffocated, hemmed in and controlled. Strangely, I felt spiritually starved. What my spirit longed for was the desert, the wide open spaces, the wilderness. My spirit wanted to have nothing and be nothing. The material comforts cluttered my life. The cultural baggage associated with being a priest, a religious and a teacher crippled me. I could not live out the expectations society had of me in these roles. It was not that I regretted joining the order, or being ordained. These to me were necessary steps in the commitment of my life to God. But I couldn't commit my life to God and then just step into the well-worn grooves of the priests and religious who lived their lives before me. The longing in me was to step out of those grooves. To get off the track altogether. To go out into the wilds where there were no tracks.

My first attempt at moving into the wilderness was in the summer of 1981. I got on a bicycle, with a tent and a sleeping-bag, and I headed for the wilds of Donegal. For six weeks I wandered the hills and valleys, the shores and headlands, filling my lungs with fresh air and my mind with fresh thoughts. Each night I pitched my tent in some field and each morning I awoke to a new day, not knowing what it would bring or in which direction I would go. After the six weeks, I came back feeling clearer in my mind, strong and confident. Nonetheless, I was quickly back into the grooves of being a priest, religious and teacher. Nothing fundamental had changed.

Then, in the following summer, I visited Aran. This was to be the most significant experience of my life. It was my first visit to the Aran Islands and I had no anticipation of what I was to experience. Ostensibly, my purpose for going there was to bring a group of young people on a holiday. The choice of Aran was arbitrary. We chose it because the school where I taught had made a trip to the island that Easter. The group who travelled there were able to tell us about it and give us the contacts.

We went to Aran for two weeks, a group of about fifteen young people and myself. All of us were involved in a youth prayer group in the town of Dundalk. We had wanted to take a holiday together that year. We stayed on the island of Inismór for two weeks. We were camping in a field near the shore, where the facilities were basic – a mobile home placed in the middle of a field equipped with a toilet and a tap. For the two weeks we were there, there was hardly anyone else on the camp-site.

That experience changed my life. It was as if the haze suddenly lifted from around me and I knew what I had to do with the rest of my life. I was to move to live on Aran. Here was the wilderness I desired. This was to be my place of resurrection. I was to leave all and go to this place.

My experience was a deep intuition. It was not rational. When I went home, I could not explain it to others. This was something I had to do. I had almost total certainty. To test it, I took time out for nine days. I let the idea sit for a while, to see if it would stay or go away. It stayed. On the ninth day, the feast of the Assumption, 15 August, I wrote a shaky letter to my superior asking for permission to go to live on Aran. Needless to say, the answer was no.

For the next two-and-a-half years, my intuition to go to Aran was tested inside and out, upside and down until I felt completely exhausted. The first test was to be told that I was to remain teaching in the same school for another year, exactly as I had been – to see if my idea would simply go away. It didn't. The second test was, the following year, to take a transfer to another job in another location – to see if that would settle me. It didn't. The third was to consult with an experienced counsellor who deals specifically with people from religious orders who are in spiritual crisis – to see if I was suffering from some delusion or psychological illness. I wasn't. The fourth was to consult with the most respected spiritual counsellors available – to see if my call was authentic. They all said it was.

From all of these tests I emerged intact, with my conviction stronger than ever. All that I knew was that I should go to live on Aran and bring none of the institutional trappings with me.

A friend came to me one day and said she had something to give me. She said she was frightened about giving it to me. She had tried to do so twice before and had lost confidence at the last minute. What she gave me was a religious poster the size of a postage stamp, stuck onto a card. The picture on it was of a small harbour with little boats tied up in it. In the background was the wide open sea. The caption on the poster said: 'Boats are safe in a harbour, but this is not what boats are made for'.

That little poster, which I carried around in my pocket for years afterwards, said it all. At a time when I was beginning to question my own sanity, when my mind was raging like a mighty storm, this little card threw me an anchor, a tangible sign from heaven. Here was exactly what I felt. I felt enclosed in a safe harbour, in this institutional, well-defined life. Everything in me screamed to leave and get out into that wild open sea – to travel to where no land was visible, to experience storms and high seas, to allow myself to be lost so that I could also be found. My call was the call of St Brendan. To go on a personal voyage in search of the land of heaven. It was also the call of Abram.

In the autumn of 1984 the tide suddenly turned. The resistance I had experienced for two years began to recede. Circumstances worked in my favour. The retreat house to which

I had been transferred a year previously was to be closed and sold. By January I would be out of a job. I asked for six months leave to go to Aran. To my surprise I got it. Subject to the approval of the local bishop and local parish priest, I could go. These approvals were granted and I arrived on Aran on 9 January 1985.

The parish priest got out of his sick-bed to collect me at the pier. He brought me to my rented accommodation in the middle of the island. It was a small thatched cottage with one tap and an outside toilet. It suited me fine. I had three rooms and three beds to choose from.

I immediately set about making myself at home and creating a new rhythm of life. This rhythm was to be the monastic rhythm of prayer, work and study. I was going to be a hermit, a Celtic monk. I joined the local people for Mass every morning in the church next door – celebrated by the local curate. I walked every foot of the island and familiarised myself with each of the holy places. I got to know my neighbours and began to speak in Irish, brushing up on school Irish long gone rusty.

My greatest learning in those days took place not from reading books, but from adjusting to a new life. I learned how to cook for myself and bake bread. My neighbour Tom took me in hand and taught me how to plant potatoes, making lazy beds to put them in and fertilising them with seaweed. Later I learned how to ride a donkey and skin a rabbit for my dinner. Other types of learning were to follow.

From the beginning, my intention was to practise hospitality. I was a hermit with only three walls to my cell. The fourth wall was missing, to allow openness to the world. Hospitality for me meant being open to the possibility of other people wanting to stay with me for a while or even to live with me. These people could be people on their own Abramic journeys, or they could be people in need.

Things began to happen much sooner than I thought. By Easter two men had come to live with me. By June, we had a further two women join us. These were all young people seeking to live the Gospel in their lives and searching for an authentic way to do it. They were looking for their place of resurrection.

My six months permission to live on Aran was extended by a further six months. Over the summer, many people came to visit, and regularly there were twelve or fifteen people around the dinner table. By September we had a further increase in numbers living in the house and things were getting a bit out of hand.

During this first year, my ability to cope with such an open policy was severely tested. On occasions I escaped into negative moods where a dark cloud would hang over me for days and I would hardly speak to anyone. I had never lived with people so closely before, despite having living in a religious community for fourteen years. Furthermore, I had never lived with women. The sexual and emotional dynamics of a mixed household were something completely new to me. Although I was floundering and not in control, I knew that this was good for me. I knew I was growing. This was life in the open sea. I was being challenged to grow in areas where I had experienced very little growth in the past – in the area of relationships and in the area of my own emotions.

One year became two years. In the second year, I built a little wooden hut for myself outside the cottage. This became my cell. It was 10 ft by 8 ft and gave me room for a bed and desk. I was working on the Irish monastic model – of a monk having his own cell. It was only later I was to discover that often two or three monks shared a one-roomed cell. Not for me. To survive in the long term, I felt I needed some space. The cottage was often packed with people and it was so small there was no way of escaping from it. The cell was to do with survival.

By this stage a daily rhythm had developed. We prayed together morning and evening. One of the small bedrooms in the cottage was converted into a prayer room. We sat on the floor and lit a candle, produced guitars and tin whistles and whatever other instruments were in use, and created a prayer session that lasted on average half an hour. At first, we stuck very closely to the Divine Office format for Morning and Evening Prayer, reciting some of it in Irish. As time went by, we became more spontaneous. Although the structure remained much the same, the content was broadened to include more personal sharing, the readings were taken from sources other than the Bible. Poetry, literature and story-telling combined with singing, spontaneous praise and silence provided a daily diet that nourished us all.

Meanwhile our days were spent working on the land or at various arts and crafts. Each person who stayed had their own personal projects on which they spent part of their day. Other parts of the day were spent working communally. Each evening we gathered for dinner, cooked by each of us in turn. Our food was vegetarian and consisted mostly of our own produce. We incorporated rice and dried beans of various kinds into the menu, the beans providing protein. In this way, we ate in solidarity with the poor of the world.

On Wednesdays and Fridays we fasted. We adopted the early Irish tradition of fasting. This tradition was based on the notion of postponing your first meal of the day. The word 'breakfast' comes from this. On Wednesdays we breakfasted at around 2.00 p.m. On Fridays we held the fast until 6.00 p.m or later, eating only one meal on this day. However, these fasts were also influenced by other circumstances. If a fast day fell on a feast day then the feast day took precedence and the fast was cancelled. Also, the demands of hospitality had priority over those of fasting. The arrival of new guests to the house cancelled whatever fast was going on at the time. Everybody ate to celebrate the arrival of the visitor. Sundays were always feast days. Whoever cooked dinner on a Sunday was asked to do something special and to provide a dessert. In this way we lived healthily and provided a balanced rhythm to our week.

Things developed from there. More people came and wanted to stay, so we developed a back door policy as well as a front door policy. While the front door policy offered hospitality and welcomed people in, the back door policy provided a way for them to move on or find their own accommodation on the island. Over time, many people chose to settle on the island and found their own accommodation. This created a network of 'blow-ins' who, while integrating into the local community, still found support among themselves. There was never a question of us forming a 'community' or separate entity from the main community of the island. All of us had come to the island to get away from being caught up in institutional or mainstream living. The last thing we needed was to set up our own institution or 'community'. But in trying to live differently and follow our dream, we did need support.

From very early on I was joined by Tess Harper. As other people came and went, she stayed on. Apart from her, the longest anybody has stayed in the house has been two to three years. Tess has become a feminine anchor for the house, to balance my masculine energy. In terms of the Celtic monastic model, Tess is the abbess, although this image is not to her liking. However, it fits with the early Irish practice of having mixed monasteries. In Kildare, Brigid's monastery was mixed and she had Bishop Conleth as her abbot. We are not trying to create a new monastery, but we are trying to live in the spirit of Irish monasticism.

With Tess as guardian of the house and of the vision alongside myself, we have been able to take on many things that otherwise would have been too much for me. From the beginning, people came to the house who were on the edge. These were not people who were choosing to be on the edge, but people who found themselves there and who needed support. It began when a friend of mine in Dublin, who worked on a project with young people in Dublin's inner city, contacted me and asked me if we would take a teenage girl who needed to be rescued from the situation she was in and given a chance in a new environment. When she came to us, she was seventeen, depressed and listless. But the rural environment suited her. She was particularly good with animals. After a while she blossomed and eventually rented her own accommodation on the island and got a job in the local factory. She now lives in Galway and has three children.

We have not always been so successful. Many people thought that if they came to Aran they could overcome their deepest problems. At first, we too were equally naive and took on all comers. However, over time we began to see where our limits lay. Unless we were going to dedicate ourselves totally to supporting people with certain problems, then we had to limit and select who we took on.

Over time, and after many different experiences, we realised that we were not able to offer much help to people with severe behavioural problems or psychiatric illnesses. Over a period, a number of recovering alcoholics had come to live with us thinking they would be permanently healed. It never seemed to work out that way. Similarly, we had people with psychiatric illnesses coming to us and thinking that they could throw away their tablets after a short while. But unfortunately it was not so. We realised that unless we were to dedicate ourselves and our home totally to supporting and accompanying these people through a healing process, we would not be of much use to them. We now will not usually take on somebody like this, but we may be able to direct them somewhere where they will get help.

However, we discovered that we could be of support to some people. Over the years, we have had stay with us a number of young people in their late teens who were coming out of institutional care and were not ready to face the world alone. Living with these young people through these transitional periods has brought us in touch with the results of parental neglect, violence in the home, sexual abuse and society's abandonment of these young people. It has also connected us with people and organisations working on their behalf in the cities.

We have also found that we can give support and some reprieve to people working with marginalised people. Very often these workers are under great pressure and suffer from exhaustion and burnout. Aran is a place of exquisite beauty and a sojourn with us away from the hustle and the hassle can provide a healing for both body and soul. There is no television in our house and as a result plenty of time is given over to conversation. Physical work on the land can reconnect people with the sources of life, and long walks along the bóithríns, beaches and cliffs can blow away the debris in the mind to give clarity of thought and vision. Prayer together in the evening is a way of acknowledging the presence of the divine in all that we experience. It allows us to share our deeper thoughts and feelings and to display the fruits of God's work within us – healing, acceptance, insight, peace of mind.

Others whom we have been able to support are those whose lives have hit a major turning point. People who have spent twenty years or more heading in one direction can find, all of a sudden, that they do not wish to travel, or are blocked from travelling, in this direction any more. For some it is a crisis within their professional careers, for others it is caused by a death or the ending of a relationship. Often these people are left in mid-life with very little and are so wounded that they are unable to see clearly what direction they must take next. A period with us has often proved helpful, and people in this situation have stayed anything from a week to a year.

But at the end of the day, we are only a small household. We cannot take on all the problems of the world and hope to solve them. Opening our home to those who experience marginalisation has been a blessing for us because it has connected us to the crucified Lord in a tangible way. It has also rooted us in reality so that our home on the island never becomes an ivory tower cut off from the realities of life in this modern world. Despite the fact that we live in such a remote area, we are, none the less, through these people, in touch with some of the major justice issues in our society.

Our rule of thumb has been to have a place in our home for one person at a time who needs special support. This way we are not diverted from our main work, which is to create a spiritual way of living that responds to the signs of the times and is right for today.

We have often thought that many families and households throughout Ireland could do what we do. If they did, the number of places required in institutional care would be greatly reduced. Of course, there are many homes already where children are fostered. But I am thinking about something broader than fosterage, to include teenagers, young adults, old people, people with physical or mental handicaps and people in transition.

There are many happy homes in Ireland that are not overstretched and that have room at their table and in their hearts for people worse off than themselves. The living out of our commitment to follow Christ takes on a very tangible reality when we open ourselves to the presence of a person in need. No institution can be an adequate substitute for a happy home where people feel they belong. To limit our homes to our own flesh and blood diminishes the power of the Gospel to change our lives.

In the past, before there was such a thing as institutional care, Christians practised the virtue of hospitality often to a heroic degree. In Ireland, the example was set by the Celtic monks for whom rules of hospitality were very strict and had the highest priority. The stranger at the gate or the person in need was to be treated as a Christ figure or an angel carrying a message. Hospitality was practical. Before anything else, the guest was to be offered three things: a footbath, a bed of clean hay with a lantern, and a good meal.

Unfortunately, the word *hospitality* has mutated today into *hospital, hostel* and *hospice*. These institutions have commandeered the word and the idea of hospitality, and have changed its meaning to suit themselves. Hospitality today has come to mean professional care or else it has come to mean tourism. 'Céad míle fáilte', as an expression of Christian hospitality, was never meant to mean 'Your need is my opportunity to make a living', no more than it was meant to mean 'You will be good for my business'. The full meaning of Christian hospitality cannot be expressed from within the context of an institution, a profession, or a business.

There is plenty of scope for a revival of Christian hospitality, one that is not tainted with the self-centredness of tourist facilities or professional care. This hospitality will take place in people's homes. Christian households will dedicate their surplus energy, space and money to caring for someone in need of a home and a supportive environment. Institutions, while they may offer some type of support and service, are never the ideal solution. No institution can offer the sense of being at home, and of being loved and cared for, that comes from true hospitality in a Christian household.

Christian hospitality has, in truth, been hijacked and then distorted by institutionalism, professionalism and tourism. It is time for those who seriously wish to follow Christ to recognise what has happened. In the story of the man on the road to Jericho, who was attacked by robbers and left dying, it was neither the institutions nor the professionals (the priest and the Levite) who picked him up, but the one who saw in him his neighbour. A revival of Christian hospitality will subvert the institutions and the professions, and will give Christian homes a distinctive and recognisable flavour.

An Charraig (The Rock) is the name of my home. It will never be an institution. Nor, I hope, will it ever be so subverted by the values of modern society as to make it impossible to live the Gospel in it. It is a place where we experiment with combining the demands of the Gospel with the signs of the times and the resources of the locality. What we have come up with is a way of life that is rooted in our Celtic tradition and tries to give that tradition an authentic expression for today. In relating to others, to nature and to God we are looking for 'right relationship', a way of living spiritually in our environment that is respectful, compassionate, non-violent, just and ecologically sensitive. Our goal is to work for transformation – transformation of ourselves, our society and our Church. We can only try. We leave God to do the rest.

I Hear God Laughing

Edwina Gateley

When I was growing up I wanted to be a missionary. At that time I was trying to follow what I call the God of the belly button. I believe that God lives about three inches in from the belly button. I think that we have made God the God of the head, rational, intellectual, a God who is separate from us, who is far away from us. But women, particularly now, are in a position to get back in touch with the God who lives in our gut, with a God who lives right within our bellies.

I went to Africa when I was twenty-one as a volunteer missionary. It was Africa that turned me upside-down. I had learned about God, about religion, about Church, and I was taking my God to the poor black folk in the bush. I wanted to empower them. I wanted to tell them about my God who was western, male and white and, obviously, British. I took my God with me to help those folk in Africa – but God was already in the people, in the villages, in the banana plantation, in the mud villages, in the poverty and simplicity and generosity of those gentle people whom I had come to save, to convert. I spent three years in Africa and then I returned to England. For a year I tried to get back into the normal stream of life. It is not my problem that two-thirds of the world lives in poverty, I thought.

But God comes when you want to be alone. God lifts a chair and places it next to mine. This God sits down and waits next to us and moves at our pace. We move as far as we permit God.

I wrote down a list of what was to become the basis of a lay missionary movement. I gave up my teaching job and I gave up my flat. For eighteen months I went around with my piece of paper. I made an appointment with the cardinal in London. I was only twenty-four and I was dressed in a mini-skirt. The cardinal asked me was I trying to start a new order. Was I trying to start a secular order? I said, No, no. In any case he gave me no authority to start a lay mission in Britain, so I went back to Africa to the people who love me exactly as I am.

God gives each one of us an instrument to dig with where we are and God scatters the seed in the soil that we have been digging. I got a letter saying that I was given a house in London and £6,000. I decided to call my movement the Volunteer Missionary Movement. I began to get letters from nurses, doctors, plumbers, farmers. One person came to join me and he asked, How many members do you have in the movement? I do not have anybody, I said, only you and me. He stayed. He was followed by another twenty-two men and women who came forward that year to be missionaries. Before long we were five hundred men and women in twenty-six countries all over the world.

Then I decided to go to America to study. I had never studied religion. I wanted to know what was being done in those big buildings. I went to the seminary and I came out with a masters in theology. I said to God, Maybe they will let me preach. But God said, Put it away. You don't need that just now. Why don't you just relax? Why don't you sit down and listen? Why don't you spend some time with me?

It was a frightening invitation. I got myself an old trailer and put it in the forest, planning to live a life of solitude and simplicity. I sat in this forest waiting for revelation. I fasted three times a week. I waited and I waited. I began talking to the squirrels. I thought I was going crazy. I felt guilty and useless. I could not pray. Nine months passed.

Then suddenly it was like God was real. God was in my belly button. I thought of a woman receiving the seed of life in her womb in conception. The seed of life requires darkness and silence. It requires warmth, and it is all so secret. And slowly, slowly the new life comes into being. And then in the ninth month, in its fullness, the birth comes.

God's word is like that too. God's word matures in our darkness, in our loneliness, our very vulnerability. At times I wondered how close I was to an abortion, not a physical abortion, but a spiritual abortion. How often do we abort God's word because we cannot wait? We are accustomed to seeing results, to keeping the pace going, to having a goal. This God has no goals; this God has no target; this God has no timing. This God sits and waits, slowly empowering the kingdom to mature in us as a child matures in her mother's womb.

The call that I heard in the forest in that ninth month was not the call I wanted. When I had gone to the forest I made a list of things that I could do: I could teach, I could go back to Africa, I could go back to England, and so on. I gave the list to God and I said, God, choose one.

But God chose something that was not on my list. It was a call to work with the very poor, with the very marginalised, a call to work with sexually abused women, prostitutes. I don't know anything about prostitutes, I protested. I am a Catholic lay woman. I am an artist. I am a poet. I don't like big cities. I could not be going into those bars. They could put a knife in your back in places like that! And what would my mother say! And anyway, look at my degree, God. There are not many women with a degree like this. I could be really useful. But God just said, I want you to work with the prostitutes.

You know, you should never go into the forest. And you should never listen deeply, because sometimes when you do that you hear things you would never normally hear. God's whisper might take you on a route fraught with all kinds of new things and you will never be the same again.

Once Jesus went off into the hills to pray and left the disciples in the boat rowing away on the lake against the storm and having a hard time. The next day he came down from the hills, and he started walking on the water. The disciples thought he was a ghost. Jesus said, Come on, I dare you, and Peter, the impetuous one, jumped out of the boat into the water and started running towards the dream, towards the call, towards Jesus of Nazareth, following his belly button, following his heart, following his dream. But suddenly he began to think, What am I doing? I am walking on water! But oh! I can't walk on water!

The moment we begin to rationalise the Kingdom, the dream fades. We ask, Is it possible to have peace on earth? Not the way the United States are building nuclear submarines and nuclear warheads! Is it possible to feed the world? Not the way we eat steak and hamburgers! Is it possible to have justice in our society? Not the way we run our governments!

If we get caught up in the rational and in facts and statistics, we may lose hope. But if we see the dream, believe in the vision and follow it, then it *is* possible to walk on water. When Peter started thinking too hard, he said, I can't do it, I can't do it. That's how I felt. Who is going to pay my medical insurance? Who is going to hire me? Who is going to pay my way? Can I go to the cardinal archbishop of Chicago and say, I feel called by God to work with prostitutes in the city of Chicago? Would you please pay me a salary?

We will never call forth the Kingdom if we get caught up in questions like, Will this work? What are the rules? What will happen? We have to follow our instinct and allow God's miracles to be revealed, and they are only revealed when we get to the edge of the cliff. I knew that the best thing was not to think, that the best thing was just to go ahead and say, Okay, I do not understand God and it is all right not to understand God. The important thing is to accept our calling, and to pursue it, even if the world says we are mad. They said that of Jesus of Nazareth. They said that of all the prophets: They are mad, they are crazy, they don't think. But they are always the ones who break through, crack, crack, crack, bringing forth the Kingdom.

So I went to Chicago, following my belly button, expecting and believing that God would take care of the insurance and the housing and everything and my job would be to go and look for the prostitutes. The first night I went out onto the streets and there I found the women on one particular street corner standing there, as we all know prostitutes do, swaying their hips, swaying their jewellery, wearing their short skirts and their high-heeled boots. There they were, flagging down the cars and seducing these poor innocent men who just happened to be driving up the road at midnight.

There they were, and I froze when I saw them. I said to God, Are these the ones that I have been called to reach out to and offer a glass of water? And I went up to them and I said, Hi! and they looked at me and they said, F... off.

Well, I got the heck out of there as fast as I could. Nobody ever said that to me before. Even in Africa they never told me to f... off, they said, Thank you for coming, Edwina, we love you. They gave me bananas and hens and goats and they loved me. But here I was trying to be faithful to my mission in the streets of Chicago and they tell me to f... off. It is not like being in church where you have a supportive congregation. They don't say things like that to you.

I said to God, You know what you can do with your prostitutes. But this God never gives up, this God said, Go back! So the next night I went back. There they were on the street corners still seducing these innocent men. Standing there doing their thing and flagging down the cars and I went up to them and I said, Hello!

Hey baby, they said, we told you to f... off. Who the f... are you anyway? You a cop?

No, I am not a cop.

You a journalist? Are you writing about us? Are you a nun?

No, I am not a nun. I am an alien, I have this card from the United States Immigration Office. I have this big blue card and it says on the front 'resident alien'.

The prostitutes then said, She ain't nobody baby, she one of them aliens. And I heard God laughing. When we have nothing, when we have no status, when we have no boxes any more, when we just have ourselves and our open hearts then God moves in with God's power: I will show you my ways if you are prepared to make an idiot of yourself.

The prostitutes know what it is like to be marginalised, they know what it is like to be nobody. So for me the very thing which I thought was a problem – I am nobody, I have no status, I don't have any money, I do not have any programme, I do not have anything to offer you – for me with these women, because I was no threat to them, my apparent drawbacks were my way into the world of prostitution. They were not threatened by me because I did not come with great authority. And they said, So you want to know what it is like to be a hooker? You want to know what it is like to do what we do on these streets? You just come and we will show you around.

And suddenly I was scared. It was the women who took me by the hand and became my teachers. I discovered in these women something I had never been told before. I had watched films and I read books about tough, hostile hookers in the bars, on the streets and in the brothels, violent, angry women, who never gave a damn about anybody, the kind of women about whom we would say, There is a tart, there is a tramp, there is a hooker. But I found, as I walked with the women, as I spent that first year on the streets of Chicago in 1983, as I got to know them, that little by little they took off their masks of anger and violence, and underneath I found the children.

Underneath I found the little girls who were raped from the age of three, five, six, seven, eight, nine, ten. Ninety-four per cent of the tough, hostile hookers on the streets of our cities and in our bus stations, train stations, in our bars, brothels and jails, were originally raped or molested or treated violently as children. The end result is a hooker with zero self-esteem.

What happens when a ten-year-old is raped consistently in her childhood? She is not going to be the headmistress of a school, she is not going to be the president of a college, she is going to say, I don't give a damn about myself or about anyone else. I don't give a damn, so I might as well do it. They press the self-destruct button and the only way they can survive is the game of pretending, the game of masquerading, the game of I-don't-care, the game of violence, and underneath there is the child who was never loved, who was never held.

But when we look at the hooker, we don't ask, Why are you selling your body on the streets, little girl? We don't go back to the original sin, the real original sin – rape, violence against the poor, violence against women. Instead, we just see the end result – prostitute. We say, Look at her, put her in jail, lock her up, harass her, laugh at her. With our laws, we compound rape, we compound incest. When I got through to the women, they began to take off their masks. They were free to cry. They were free to be themselves. They had me with them and I could hold them and I could say, It's okay, sweetheart, it's okay, baby. They could cry, and they would tell me how they were raped by their daddy, or their granddaddy or their brother or their cousin or their uncle or whoever it was. And for the first time in their lives these women from the streets of Chicago had somebody who would just hold them and understand them instead of rape them or beat them or condemn them.

And I said to myself, why did I get into this? There are too many for me. There are between 25,000 and 60,000 prostitutes in Chicago alone and I am only a little Catholic laywoman. I can't handle this. It was like I had touched the tip of an iceberg and it was beginning to burst open. And God was saying, I dare you to take care of the children, I dare you to look at things a little bit differently, I dare you to look underneath instead of at the outside.

One night I walked down a street very late at night. I knew I was supposed to go into this tavern, that for some reason it was important to be there that night. So I went into that tavern, in this dirty back street in Chicago. It was an old, rundown kind of tavern and I opened the door and inside it was dark, but I could hear the music. I found my way up to the front, to the bar counter, and I climbed on a bar stool and asked the barman for a glass of wine. I sat there with my glass of wine and I said to myself, What the hell am I doing here, in this dirty place at midnight, in this area? What am I doing here? But my gut told me it was all right. Then the door opened and in came a woman. She found her way to the counter where I was and she climbed onto the bar stool next to me. She banged her fist on the counter and she ordered a jug of wine. She seemed to be an old woman, although she was only in her fifties, but you could see she had been around a long time. She looks at me and says, 'Hi, hon.' I said, 'Hello.' She looks at me again and she says, 'Are you hungry?' I said, 'Just a little bit.' So she leant down and she put her hand in her bag and she pulled out a jumbo-sized sliced loaf and she dumped it on the counter and she opened it. She put her hand down again and she pulled out a can of tuna fish that was opened and she took a slice of dry bread and she put her fist into the can of tuna, took out a fistful of tuna and slapped it onto the dry bread. She took another slice and placed it on top and said, 'Here you are hon. I haven't eaten for three days and I have been looking for somebody to share it with. I have just stolen it from the shop around the corner.' So there I am sitting with stolen bread and tuna in this dirty bar eating it and thinking, What the hell am I doing here, God?

Then she says to me, 'You know, hon, it is so difficult to make it nowadays. I find it so hard. I only make five bucks, maybe ten bucks a day if I am real lucky. The guys are just not around as much as they used to be.'

Then she looked at me and she said, 'But you are still young. With my experience – I know where all the tricks are, I know where all the guys are – and your body, we could make a great team, hon.'

She was looking for a partner! I said, 'No, no I am awfully sorry, I am not a prostitute.' This was the first time I had apologised for not being a prostitute! She said to me, 'You're not a hooker? Then, what are you doing in here? This is a hooker bar. This is where the tricks come in and pick up the girls. You shouldn't be in here. Who are you?' I said, 'I am a Catholic minister.'

'You are a minister, hon? There has never been no minister in here, never. There never been no Christian in a place like this.' And she just put her arms around me and she sobbed and she sobbed and she began to tell me her story, her story of rape as a child, her story of violence on the streets of Chicago, in and out of jail, in and out of men's cars, all her life. She sobbed out this story. And all I did that night in that dirty bar was hold that woman. I held her and I listened to her, as, for the first time, probably, in her life she told her story and she had somebody to hold her. It was all I could do. I had no programme, no money, no solutions, no answers, nothing. But I held her.

Early that morning I left her there, and as I walked down the streets, I reflected on what had happened. I had walked into that bar looking for the Kingdom and the woman came, and she brought the bread and she broke it and she gave it to me. She took the wine and we shared it. She brought the fish and we shared it. She told me her story and broke open her heart and we shared a kiss of peace. That night in that dirty place, there had been a Eucharist. I heard God say: I will show you things that you will never otherwise see if you dare to reach out to listen to my word, because I am everywhere, everywhere.

I discovered with all the women I met on the streets of Chicago the longing to be loved, to be healed, and the need not for incarceration and judgment but for holding and embracing and for new possibilities. It was through the personal stories of the women that I began to learn so much about the pain of their journeys. Perhaps what we need to do is walk with them on their journey.

There is a story about a king's daughter who got lost in the forest and was found by a poor farmer. She lived with the farmer and learned to dig in the field. She didn't know who she was and the farmer didn't know who she was. One day she was found by the king's people and they asked her, Do you know who you are?

She said, I am the farmer's daughter, I am a potato digger. They told her she was the daughter of the king. The young woman continued to dig the potatoes, but she dug them differently. There was a difference in the way she held herself. There was a light in her eyes. She now knew who she was: she was the king's daughter.

When I see the prostitutes standing on the streets and in the jails and in the brothels, I ask, them, Do you know who you are? And they say, Yes, Edwina, we are shit. No, I say, You are the temple of the Holy Spirit. No, Edwina, we are the scum of the earth. No, you are God's work of art.

God says, Will anybody tell you who you are? It is as if God is looking for cheerleaders, looking for champions to say, Go and tell my children, go and tell those who perceive themselves as scum, go and tell them that they are mine. Slowly, perhaps, the down-trodden will come to know who they are. Maybe through our faith a woman will be able to say, I am all right, I am okay. Another day she might go so far as to say, I think I am beautiful. I am okay. I am beautiful. God breaks through.

Working in Chicago's brothels was a very painful experience. In church, we have a podium, we have a pulpit, we wear certain clothes, we have holy books, we have an audience, we are qualified to teach and we are as secure and assured. Then one day God comes along and takes away the pulpit and leaves you with nothing special to wear, and even the holy book is no longer of help. And God says, Preach my word, and you are sitting there and you think, What can I say in the brothel? You can't say, What school did you go to? How is you husband? Do you have any children? What church do you go to? Suddenly all the things that you would say in a normal context are swept away. You have nothing to say in a brothel.

You have nothing to say because you are struck dumb by the pain. You sit there, waiting for a knock on the door and a man to come in and pick a woman. You can't find conversation to fill in the time while you are sitting there with the women who are wondering, Will I be chosen? Will I be chosen for twenty minutes? Will I make ten dollars in the next twenty minutes? Will I be all right? Will my body be okay? Because I have to pay the rent and I have two kids. I really have got to make some money today.

We have preached enough. Now we must sit with the pain. Now we must sit where the people suffer and maybe our hearts, which have toughened up through the years, will soften, because we are exposed to the pain of the poor, of the prostitutes. As our hearts soften, they may become like sponges, and maybe they will soak up some of the violence. That is all we can do. It is a different method of ministry, sitting with and holding one another, knowing that we cannot solve the thing overnight.

Rusty is in her late thirties and has her hair dyed blonde and wears this low-cut blouse and has track marks all down her arms from drugs. Desperate to make a date, Rusty leaps up when a customer walks into the brothel during his lunch break from the office. She says, Hi baby, do you want to turn a date? She does a little pirouette in front of him, and the guy looks at her, and then looks around at the other women, and chooses another woman. And Rusty, who had been reading a book, sits down and hides her face behind her book, and her face drops behind it. The doorbell rings again, and Rusty is up again, and does her little dance, but the same thing happens. Three times Rusty is rejected and sits down. I am sitting near her, and I see her knuckles go white and I see her lips tremble and her eyes fill with tears. Whan all you have left is your body to sell for ten or fifteen dollars and nobody wants it, you have nothing, and you know it. What does a disciple of Jesus do in that case? All I could do was put my hand out and put it on her shoulder. Right from my little toes it came. I am sorry, I am sorry. I looked in her eyes. She knew I meant it, and that I loved her. She knew that all that I could do was reach out and touch her.

I was invited to preach in a rather large suburban middle-class church in Chicago. My friends from the brothel said they would come to church to hear me preach, so there was a whole row of prostitutes and the madam there in the middle of the congregation. I thanked them for coming, and the madam said she missed a whole morning's work but it was worth it. You know Edwina, they said, you come to us in our place of work, so we came to support you in your work. We know it is hard for you, being a woman, they really don't like you preaching. It was a powerful affirmation for me that they wanted to show solidarity with me and to support me in my struggle for feedom and justice.

As a result of seeing what was going on, I knew that we had to do something. I knew there were thousands of women on the streets. It was no good meeting them in McDonalds. It was no good trying to stop a woman killing herself or taking too many drugs, or getting beaten up by a pimp on a street corner. We had to have a place where these women could gather and where they could cry, where they could have a teddy-bear instead of a pimp to go to bed with, a place where women would not have to trade their bodies to be loved, to be held, a place where they could be safe. We needed a place where they could go to school, where I could say to them, How about being a computer technician? How about being a secretary? You can do it but you can only do it if you have people who believe in you and you know that.

I wanted to find a house for these women who would come from the jails and from the brothels and from the streets and where they would be able to turn around and say, We are not shit. We are beautiful. We know who we are. We are the daughters of the king.

I found a house, and I called it Genesis House, a place of new beginnings. Over the years, Genesis House has reached out to thousands of women who have come to the door saying, Help me! I have had enough, I want to live. I look back at the Volunteer Missionary Movement which has sent out over a thousand lay missionaries all over the world and I see Genesis House with its women in prostitution now beginning to heal and

I hear God laughing. We have moved mountains. We did it, because we dared. I am in awe of what God has done and every day I see the beauty of these women and their struggle to turn their lives around from the scum and the pits and I say, If they can do it, then we can. We too can have a dream, and we too can stand up over and against poverty and oppression. We can say, We have a dream. We can go for that dream and we can believe in miracles.

Perhaps a story of something that happened at Genesis House will serve to illustrate what we are all about and how God breaks through into our lives if we are open. In the early days, I did not really know what I was doing. The women were coming in to Genesis House from jail. They were being beaten up by pimps. I needed space. I needed a break. One evening I had no women sleeping in the house, so I decided to invite my friends for dinner. I was planning to have a chat with my friends about theology, ministry, justice, things like that, just for a change from conversations about jail, pimps and sex. There were nuns and priests and an Irish Christian Brother and we all came and gathered to have a nice quiet evening at Genesis House. Just as we were about to sit down, the doorbell rang and in came Helena, one of the women, with her hair flying and tears running down her face, saying, 'I can't take it any more, Edwina, I can't take any more, I am sick and tired of it, I just have to get out of this place.'

I said, 'Helena be quiet, I have visitors, we are eating.'

She said, 'I have not eaten either and I am so hungry.'

Then there was a bang on the door and there was her pimp, a big fellow. He came charging in shouting, 'Where is my woman?'

I said, 'Eddie, shut up, just be quiet. Right now we are having dinner. Have you eaten Eddie?'

'No, I ain't eaten.'

'Come and join us,' I said, 'you might as well.'

He sat down and not long later the doorbell rang and another two girls said 'Hi' and I said, 'Why don't you come and have dinner with us?' and they said, 'Great!'

We sat down and I knew the evening was going to be different. This Irish Christian Brother had literally walked out of the Monastery of Our Lady of the Snows. He was as pure and innocent as the driven snow. There is one thing about women in prostitution, they know exactly where you are coming from, and they know human nature very, very well. They sat opposite this Christian Brother and one of the women poked the other woman beside her and pointed at the Christian Brother and leant over and said, 'Hi! Brother, what beautiful eyes you have!'

The conversation was very different from what I had planned, but at the end of the dinner one of the women said, 'Well, we are such a happy family, why don't we go down and pray together, down into our little chapel?'

I said, 'No, no. We are not doing that tonight.'

One of the priests said, 'If the ladies want to pray that is rather nice.'

I said, 'No, no, I know these women.'

But he persisted and so we went down to the chapel downstairs and we sat around in a circle. I lit a candle and I said, 'We are going to stay here for ten minutes and if anyone wants to pray just feel free to say something.'

A little black prostitute started. She said, 'Oh Lord, you are our shepherd and we are the sheep of your flock. Hallelujah, Hallelujah.'

And the pimp said, 'Hey! Where is she coming from?'

And the Christian Brother said, 'I would like to pray now,' and he began, '*Salve Regina, mater misericordiae...*'. He sang the hymn to the Blessed Virgin in Latin.

The pimp said, 'What kind of a language is that?'

I said, 'It is a kind of sacred language; it is a Church language; don't worry about it.'

The pimp gets up, goes over to his woman and gives her a clout and says, 'Pray!'

She says, 'No.'

He gives her another belt and says, 'Pray!'

I said, 'Look, Eddie, no fighting, she doesn't have to pray if she doesn't want to.'

He said, 'She can pray. He prayed and she prayed. My woman can pray too!'

Then the prostitute said, 'I can only pray in silence.'

I said, 'Okay, why don't we all stand up and hold each other's hands and bow our heads and ask God to bless us?'

And we all stood up in that simple basement chapel. We all held hands, prostitute and priest, pimp and nun, white and black, lay and religious, we all held hands and in that moment I felt God breaking through and saying, This is the Kingdom, this is my Kingdom.

PRAYER, POLITICS AND TRANSFIGURATION

John Halsey

I: Prayer and Politics (1979)

Part I of this essay is the transcript of a talk given by Brother John Halsey to a L'Arche gathering in 1979. It is a vignette of his work and community at that time. The occasion of this meeting with L'Arche proved to be a significant moment in his community's journey.

I live in Roslin, near Edinburgh, in a small community consisting of four members, three men and a woman, called the Community of the Transfiguration, which was established in 1965.

I work as a labourer in a paint shop that was part of a garage in Edinburgh. Our works, the body shop and paint shop, is one of about six branches of the firm. The car bodies are repaired in the body shop, and then they come through to the paint shop, where they are painted by the paint-shop team. There are also cleaners who polish the cars, and then there are the mechanics and storemen. There are about thirty of us on the shop floor altogether, and seven in the paint shop.

One of my first impressions when I started working there was that I was at the bottom of the pack. I felt like the little dog listening to his master's voice on the old HMV records. I was treated like a dog, and I was shouted at like a dog. My foreman had a habit of shouting my name from the other end of the garage and expecting me to come trotting up. He would then give me instructions that I could not understand because I cannot understand the Midlothian dialect, which is very broad. To make matters worse, he would walk away from me in the course of giving me this string of instructions, so I could not hear anyway and I would have to trot behind him like a little dog, trying to make out what he was saying. The only time that I remember being treated like this before was when I was in the army. I accepted it then, as being part of army life, part of the training. But in this garage it was for real.

When I began to find my feet I saw that this attitude was not just my foreman's. It went right up to the top, to the managing director (let's call him Mr Bloggs), and it went right through the firm, this business of trampling on the person down below and keeping him there in a way that was very demeaning. Mr Bloggs is like a caricature. His nickname is the Godfather and he is just like the character in the film. He is a little fat man of about sixty-five with glasses and a buttonhole. Mr Bloggs visits our place about once or twice week and he has a peculiar way of going around talking into a little machine, as if the people working there do not exist at all. He is interested in the equipment or some of the cars, perhaps, but the people there do not exist for him. He barks at the people under him and he tramples on them. These people are his sons, directors of the company. They are treated like dogs, and then they pass it on to the other directors, and then it comes down to the manager.

After I had been there for about a month or two, I said to myself, 'You can't give in to this inhuman nonsense. Here is a human being, Mr Bloggs, who comes around and looks through people as if they did not exist. You can't let him get away with this.' So I made a resolution that the next time he came into the shop I would make it my business to pass him by and smile at him cheerily and say 'Good morning, Mr Bloggs,' and see what happened.

When I saw him coming in, I picked up a bucket of water – a paint shop labourer often has a bucket of water, that is his stock-in-trade – and I passed him. He was with the manager and walking straight towards me. I looked him straight in the eye and gave him a cheery 'Good morning,' as if it was a thing I did every day, and he stopped dead in his tracks as if I had tried to shoot him. It was extraordinary, there was absolute horror and fear on his face, and without saying a thing he then went on as though nothing had happened.

When I mentioned this to an old cleaner who works in the shop and who knew Mr Bloggs very well, he said 'I know what you mean, he looked at you as if you had got horns on.' It was clear to me that this attitude of treating people like dogs came from him. It travelled down through the firm and it had very demeaning effects. People were made to feel less than human. This sort of behaviour is not only demeaning but it is very destructive, especially at a human level.

I would sometimes be given a job to do by a painter, and then the foreman would come along and say that he wanted me to do something else. Perhaps pressure had been put on him because there was a rush on a particular car. So I would down tools on the job I was on and make a start on the new job I had been given. Then the junior manager would come along and say 'I want you off that. Will you go along and polish a car?' So I would down tools again and go off and start on that. Then the foreman would come along and ask why I hadn't finished the job he gave me. So I would have pressure coming from all sorts of places and I would not know what was going to happen next.

I had been in the army and I am fairly thick-skinned, so I could laugh at it, but there was one young laddie, a cheerful bloke and conscientious at his job, who could not stand up to this kind of pressure. One day he just left and he was taken off to a psychiatric hospital next day. Something similar happened to another skilled and conscientious worker, a panel-beater I was friendly with. The way the panel-beaters' pay works is based on incentives and bonuses, and unless he worked so many hours he did not get more than his very basic wage, which he needed for his family. His foreman was not straight, so he got the most difficult jobs, which put him in a vicious circle, forcing him onto the lowest rung, though his skill should have enabled him to be making good money. It was not just the money, though. He felt threatened and he started having worries and losing sleep. He went to his doctor and his doctor told him that this was due to worries at work and he should have a week off. When he asked the manager for this, the manager just laughed.

On my first day in this job, I asked, during the morning tea-break, while everybody was having their cups of tea and reading the paper and having their fags, 'What about a union in this place? Is there a union or what happens?' The effect of that little question was electric. It was as if the atmosphere suddenly became charged, and it took me some time to discover what was behind this. They all knew, everybody knew, that the management had them where they wanted, were behaving in a way that was not human and that they, my mates, were demeaning themselves by conniving in this treatment. They really knew that the only answer was to join a union. But they did not want to do this. None of them did. Apparently two or three years before that, two people had tried to start a union in the main branch in Edinburgh, and they were fired on the spot because the last thing the firm would tolerate was any union participation. That would be a threat to their authority. Nobody wanted to join a union because they knew that to do so would be instantly to bring down recrimination from the management. So the very mention of a union met with silence. Curiously enough, I found out later that the union did not want to know about us either, because they knew the firm Bloggs & Bloggs and they knew there would be trouble for them if the union became involved in that firm.

But we did eventually all join the union, after I had been there about two years. It had nothing to do with me personally. I am not a rabble rouser even if I wanted to be and I am not good at converting people. In fact the management did it all for us. What happened was this. When we were about to go off on our summer holidays one year, we got little notes inside our payslips with our holiday money, accusing us of not doing the amount of overtime we had said we would do. They required us to sign our names to an agreement to do overtime at least two nights each week, whenever the management wanted it, and if we did not sign this we would be breaching our contracts of employment and putting our jobs at risk. One of the paint shop workers had a friend who was a lawyer. He brought his lawyer friend into the canteen and we discussed the issue, and everybody in the shop felt so angry and threatened by what had happened that it did the trick for us and the upshot of it was that we all joined the union. Or rather, not quite all. We did not become a closed shop, which meant that we did not have all the power that sometimes goes with full union membership. When you have got a lot of power then it can be abused and you get all sorts of horrors, so I think we were quite lucky in that respect.

The management did not like this development at all and we had running battles and a series of frightful tensions and crises for about three months, after which the shop steward was sacked and the outcome of that was that I was put in as shop steward because no-one else would take the job. One of the reasons I am telling you this is that I think many people have a very stereotyped image of what sort of a person a shop steward or a union activist is, an idea that we are all anarchists, but that is very far from the truth.

When I go to my job, I go as a member of my community. This is tremendously important to me. If I hadn't been a member of my community, I wouldn't have been doing that sort of job at all, or if I had got that job, I wouldn't have stayed in it. I certainly wouldn't have been a shop steward if I wasn't a member of the community, with the community behind me, reflecting with me on the situations that cropped up. In fact there would have been no union membership in the works if I hadn't been there, and this wouldn't have happened if I hadn't belonged to my community. That is how we operate.

We are often asked, 'What's your community for?' and the answer is that our community is essentially for only one thing and that is prayer. It's a contemplative community, and we have what is called a rule. That doesn't mean we have a list of rules we have to keep. It is something that is written down, to define where we have got to move towards. Here is an extract from our rule:

> Brothers and sisters, your vocation is none other than the call of God who wills you to live to the praise of his glory, the light of that glory he has revealed in the face of Jesus Christ.

A little further on it says:

> Your calling is to a life of prayer in the world, to be at the same time united with Christ and with the world which He came to save.

So that is what our community is for, it is a contemplative community but in the world, open.

It is essentially a monastic community. We take monastic vows, renewed each year, and we pray the monastic office. We live in little hut cells, six feet by eight, in a garden enclosure outside the community building, which is an old shack. We have five of these huts, for we are often joined by friends and visitors, and then a bigger hut which is our chapel (where we have our corporate prayer, Psalms, Old Testament and New Testament and Intercessions and so forth and Eucharist more or less daily). This gives a sort of simplicity and a 'scraped-downness' to our lives.

We also have, as part of our discipline of life, built-in solitude, silence, withdrawal, one hour of adoration in silence each day. Each month, each of us has at least twenty-four hours of solitude in a hermitage hut or somewhere where we can be alone or quiet. Each year we have at least a week of this, again in a hermitage or in a contemplative community. So solitude and withdrawal are built into our life, in addition to our corporate prayer and our corporate life and of course there is the bread-winning, the work, our involvement in the world and in society which, together with hospitality, is a vital element in our lives.

The door is always open, and we have found that lots of fascinatingly different people walk through that door. The Lord has been marvellously good to us in this way. Some come to look and talk and some to stay, maybe for a night, or sometimes, by arrangement, for a week or more. Some stay as long as a year or more.

We have been pushed in two directions over the years. We have not planned this, but we have been pushed by events and, we believe, by the Lord. One direction is towards solitude and withdrawal. We have found for instance that each brother and sister having an individual hut cell is a way in which this can be practised and developed. It is not just about privacy, withdrawing from others, but it is about being where we need to be in order to bring renewal, not only for ourselves but for our community and for our world. We have learned that when we are engaged in solitude, we are with people in a new and a deeper way. It is not a question of escape. If you go into solitude with the idea of escaping then you soon find that you cannot manage it. You go to meet yourself and your God and your world and to bring them into focus. We have found that more and more people have come to share this with us – all sorts of people from all sorts of backgrounds at all sorts of levels and with all sorts of needs. People come who have not just spiritual or religious needs, but a need for real, positive solitude and quiet for their souls' health, and they are glad to have the opportunity which we try to provide. That is one direction in which we have been impelled, quite without planning or without expecting it.

The other direction is really what I started with, the direction of the world and engagement with people, not only as individuals, but in society, for example, in my own case, my involvement in union politics. If you had told me five years ago that I would be a shop steward in two or three years, I would have fled.

So we have been mysteriously pulled in these two directions, seemingly in contradiction, but in experience complementarily, in a way that we feel is very important: on the one hand, towards engagement with humanity and on the other towards solitude and the contemplative life. Perhaps this is to do with the community's prayer, and here I would like to mention two prayers we use. We conclude each morning and evening office with a prayer we have learnt from the Taizé Community:

> May the Lord keep us in the joy, the simplicity and the compassion of the Holy Gospel.

This speaks of three gifts of the Spirit manifested so clearly in the humanity of Jesus, deriving from the Blessed Trinity and to be received and lived by us.

The other prayer is the prayer of Charles de Foucauld, which you may know as the prayer of abandonment, and which we say together each day:

> Father, I abandon myself into your hands. Do with me what you will. Whatever you do I will thank you. Let only your will be done in me as in all your creatures and I will ask nothing else, my Lord. Into your hands I commend my spirit. I give it to you with all the love of my heart for I love you, Lord, and I need to give myself; to surrender myself into your hands with a trust beyond all measure because you are my Father.

When you pray that, very curious things happen. God does listen and use your prayers in a way which, when you look at it with your eyes open, is terrifying and wonderful. This is what I believe is happening in my life and in the life of my community.

The Transfiguration, the marvellous mystery of the New Testament after which our community is named, used to be a very important festival in the early days of the Church, and in the Orthodox Church it still ranks at the level of Christmas, Easter and Pentecost. But now, when the Church is celebrating this mysterious event of the Transfiguration of our Lord, on 6 August, the world remembers Hiroshima.

There is a very curious and sinister relationship between these two events, between the activity of God himself and this atom bomb which overshadows our age. The first test bomb was code-named 'Trinity', and the bomb dropped on Hiroshima was code-named 'Little Boy'. It seems as if the nuclear explosion at Hiroshima is a demonic counterpart of the Transfiguration. Hiroshima was a ghastly disfiguring in the demonic brightness of the first atom bomb, as Christ was transfigured by divine brightness. A phrase from the Hindu scriptures, 'Brighter than a thousand suns', came to Oppenheimer's mind when he saw the bomb 'Trinity' exploding.

Most of you will be familiar with the story of Jesus taking his disciples, his inner three, as it were, Peter, James and John, up the mountain, Luke tells, us to pray. He spoke to his disciples of his cross, of the exodus, of his journey that he would accomplish at Jerusalem. He was speaking of the cross and he was looking forward to the cross. Then he was transfigured before them and he became bright, dazzlingly white, whiter than any earthly whiteness. Moses and Elijah were seen with him in his glory. Then Peter said: 'It is good for us to be here, let us stay here, let's capture this moment. Let's make three tents – one for you, one for Moses and one for Elijah.' Then we are told that the cloud removed Moses and Elijah and the disciples were left with Jesus only. And also we are told about the scene at the bottom of the mountain, where the other disciples were approached by a man who was in absolute despair because his son was an epileptic, who was continually injuring himself and was now at his last gasp, and the other disciples were helpless to heal him. Eventually Jesus came down the mountain and healed this lad.

Here we see Jesus transfigured, and at the bottom of the mountain the impotent Church and the world in its desperation. On the mountain, the disciples saw only Jesus, and this speaks to us of our need for solitude and for being alone with God. It speaks to us of Jesus with his disciples and it speaks also of the human predicament regarding which the Church on its own is impotent, in which there is just desperation and the only relief comes when Jesus comes down from the mountain and the disciples turn the problem over to him. In the middle of this mysterious event is Jesus in his brightness, looking forward to and committing himself to the cross.

It seems to me that the human race, all of us, are being given the choice of two ways. We can go one way, which is ploughing along the road of power, trampling on people, barking like a dog, the way the people in my firm treated their workers. If you choose to go that way, it leads eventually to the bomb and disfiguration and unimaginable horror. The other way we can choose to go is towards Christ, in his littleness and in his suffering and in his way to the cross and in his movement down among the little people and among the poor, and that is the way to his glory. There is Christ in the dazzling brightness of his love. That is the alternative.

I believe that our century, in particular, is faced with these alternatives. The early Church used to place tremendous importance on something which we tend to forget: that the glory of Christ is not just Jesus in glory but it is the glory to which we are all moving, to which the Church in Christ and the whole human race in Christ is moving. This glory is for us. And the way to this glory is through the cross. And so the Transfiguration speaks to us of the past, the present, the future. It speaks to us of everything and it speaks particularly to us in this century.

II: Transfiguration (1996)

In this addendum, written recently, Brother John gives a brief summary of the origins of his community and how he came to join it.

Our little community has its roots in a project that was started in Sheffield by the late Dr Leslie Hunter, then the Anglican bishop of Sheffield. In 1957 he commissioned Roland Walls (then an Anglican priest at Cambridge, now Brother Roland, a Roman Catholic priest, who is still a member of our community) to explore the possibility of training men for the ordained ministry in the light of the Gospels, as an 'apostolic' community. They shared all aspects of life in community, attending especially to the words of Jesus and so trying to discover existentially what 'Follow me' means for us today, in the context of the Sheffield working world and the worldwide Church of the 1950s.

Up to that time, my personal journey could be said to have been in the mould of 'ordinary life', if ordinary life can be said to include one so exceptionally privileged as mine. After public school, two years' national service in the army and three at university, I was working in Canada when I felt called to change track and move towards the ordained ministry in the Church of England.

Soon after starting at theological college in preparation for my ordination, I heard about Brother Roland's 'Sheffield Twelve', as the project at Sheffield was called, and which had just started up, so I volunteered and was accepted for the following year. For the first part of the year, I and my fellow-students (there were six of us) found manual jobs in industry (for me, as for most of us, in a steelworks) and lodgings in the homes of working people, which enabled us to share their lives. For the second part of the year we lived together as a household/community, with the single aim of study and reflection on the contemporary world and Church, seen in the light of the Gospels. Each day started with prayer and then an hour's study of the Gospels. In our studies we learned about such people and groups as Charles de Foucauld, Bonhoeffer and his Finkelwalde underground seminary, Mission de France and the French worker-priests, and Jacques de Loew and his missionary worker teams in Marseilles. We were in contact with the Little Brothers of Jesus, Taizé, the Iona Community and others drawn to community life in solidarity with the poor. For all of us, it was an experience both radical and seminal.

After this I returned to complete my more formal training for ordination, was duly ordained, and worked as a curate in the parish near Sheffield where I had lived and worked in the steel mill two years previously. After four years, it was time for me to move on, but where was God calling me to go?

The answer came out of an invitation to a conference from Bishop Hunter, who was now retired, and who had gathered around him for twenty-four hours a strange assortment of (mostly) eccentric clergy from all over Britain. Among them was Brother Roland, who had by this time ended up at Roslin (which is another story, and one that is his, not mine, to tell). The upshot was, briefly, that two of us at that conference agreed to start out with Brother Roland as the Community of the Transfiguration on the feast of the Transfiguration, 6 August 1965, under the wing of the Anglican bishop of Edinburgh.

My journey since then has been the journey of our little community, and since our coming together with the L'Arche community on the occasion of the talk that is transcribed as the first part of this essay, L'Arche's journey has also been very much part of ours. I believe that defining moments on our journeys of faith are given to us to clarify and deepen our vocation.

> Ours is none other than the glory which you gave to me and I have given them; that they may be one, even as we are one: with me in them and you in me, may they be so completely one that the world may realise that it was you who sent me and that I have loved them as much as you loved me.
> (John 17: 22ff)

A Personal Journey

Peter McVerry

My growing up was a pretty normal affair, that is to say, I was sheltered from realities which were not a feature of the social class to which I belonged. I grew up in a small provincial town and we lived a comfortable, but not luxurious life. I was aware of people living in local authority flats in poor surroundings, but I was not aware that although they lived only a mile or two away, their lives were a thousand light-years away from mine. Like all children, I thought the world was the same for everyone.

Life in the seminary in those days was an equally sheltered existence. Involvement in activities and with groups outside the seminary was positively discouraged or at least monitored and controlled. The occasional 'pastoral experience' in the local youth club did not seriously interfere with the life of illusion.

It was in 1974, when I was thirty, that the bubble burst. The Jesuits had been given a new direction, which focused on the promotion of justice as an integral part of our preaching the Gospel. We knew that our lifestyle and ministry were almost exclusively middle-class and that we were unaware of the effects of poverty and injustice on those who were marginalised in our society. The promotion of justice could not take place from a comfortable armchair.

With two other Jesuits, I volunteered to live and work in the inner city. This 'insertion experiment' was a new experience for us Jesuits and so what was expected from us was not clearly defined. Nobody could tell us what we should be doing. We were free to do what we felt had to be done.

We were given a top floor flat by Dublin Corporation in a terraced house which had been divided like all the other houses in the street into eight flats. Luckily it was a dry weekend when we moved in. When it rained, the rain came through the ceiling and dripped down from the electric light bulb in the middle of the room. At night, lying in bed, you could hear the rats in the ceiling above running, fighting, squealing, dragging things along the floor – bits of food, probably – and occasionally gnawing through the electric wires. Sometimes the lights would go out and you knew another rat had met a shocking end. Families on the ground floor would tell you stories of waking up in the morning and finding a rat on the baby's cot. The rats were as big as kittens, immune to every poison invented.

But the worst thing was the sound-proofing – there was none. We could hear the news on the television in the flat below us perfectly clearly. Every noise or conversation could be overheard. Now there were many very fine families living in Summerhill in those days. Many residents had grown up in the area as had their parents and grandparents before them and they had no interest in moving somewhere else. Their relationships with their extended family and their friendships from childhood were more important to them than the physical conditions in which they lived. But those conditions were very harsh.

However, some other people were living there because they had been evicted from other areas for non-payment of rent or because of other problems. Often these residents had personal or relationship problems which caused their eviction in the first place. These problems were not solved by eviction, of course, simply relocated. In some cases, fierce arguments and fights between husband and wife would erupt in the middle of the night and go on for hours until they fell asleep from drink and exhaustion. But the whole house was kept awake. The absence of any sound-proofing between the flats meant that everyone was awake and hearing every move. Perhaps two or three nights in a row you might get very little sleep. And if you had to get up for work in the morning, or get up to go to school, you might sleep it out and lose your job, or miss days from school.

I had had no idea that people lived in such difficult and

oppressive conditions in the very same city which provided me with a very comfortable lifestyle. It was a learning experience that radically changed me. I was turned upside-down and inside-out. Views and judgements I considered common-sense were seen to be the products of limited experience, a narrow database and defence mechanisms. I found terrific goodness and immense ability in people whom employers wouldn't touch, in children who couldn't cope with school and got expelled, hanging round the corners, unemployable, without a penny in their pockets and ending up in crime, labelled by the media – and not so long before, by me – as 'thugs', 'wasters', 'no-goods'. 'Respectable' people wrote letters to the papers calling for the introduction of the birch, harsher prison conditions, the return of the Garda 'heavy gang'.

I had discovered goodness in those whom others thought evil and I was discovering what appeared to me now to be evil in those who considered themselves good. My conventional values were questioned, sometimes rejected and newer, less conventional values replaced them.

It became clear that young people were a very neglected group in the inner city. Many of them had left school very early, sometimes as young as nine, and were hanging around with no skills, no future and the certainty that Mountjoy Prison lay ahead.

We set up a youth club in our own flat. The youth club became a craft centre where young people made 'pin-and-thread' pictures. We sold their products door-to-door all over Dublin, and the whole enterprise was phenomenally successful. The young people not only experienced a sense of achievement sometimes for the first time in their lives but were able to earn money to go on trips, buy fishing rods, get guitar lessons, whatever it was they wanted to do. Well-off people in comfortable surroundings actually valued and wanted what these inner-city kids had created.

From the profits, we set up a leather workshop. The same

young people made leather belts, purses and armbands that others valued and were prepared to pay for. Their leather belts were sold in the big Dublin department stores. But the kids couldn't get in to see their own belts being sold, because the security men saw them as potential shop-lifters and kicked them out.

Some of these young people knew only pain and meaninglessness. 'God put me in this world to suffer,' one of them used to say to me regularly. That was the only reasonable explanation for his situation that he could come up with. How could I talk to him about God?

Many of them didn't want to believe in God. The message they got all the time from the society in which they lived, was that they were no good, useless, trouble, unwanted. After a while, a very short while, you come to believe it's true what they say and think you are no good, useless, unwanted. So, if there is a God, then God too sees them as no good, useless, and unlovable. It's bad enough having to go through life being made to feel no good and unwanted, but to have to go through eternity being made to feel no good and unwanted was too much to bear. So the Good News for these young people was that there is no God.

In our work, we were aware of some young people, almost all boys, who were sleeping rough, in the local bus depot or in derelict buildings. There were not many of them, too few to categorise as 'homeless children'. They oscillated between home and the streets. On visiting their homes it became very clear why they did not live there: serious problems such as alcoholism, violence and rejection were very much in evidence. Children might have to wait till one in the morning for their parents to return from the pub and then have to sit through a long, drunken argument between them, always getting hurt emotionally and sometimes physically in the process. There were children from houses where there was no food and who had to fend for themselves on the streets, children with no electricity at home so that it was brighter and more interesting outside on the street.

Robbing cars and snatching handbags were their 'work experience'. They were children who lived on the street, and lodged at home only occasionally, when it was convenient for them, but had few ties to anywhere or anyone. Conventional youth services were not very useful to them.

At one of the regular meetings between voluntary youth workers in the area, I proposed starting a small hostel for some of these boys. Along with two other projects – an educational project for children who had dropped out of school and a recreational project for teenagers who were at risk – the proposal went to the Department of Health. They were all accepted and funding was promised. It would be nice to think that the department agreed because they saw the need for and value of these projects, but the reality was very different. It was political expediency that ensured funding for these projects: night after night, the evening papers had headline stories of cars being robbed and handbags being snatched in the Summerhill/Gardiner Street/Sean McDermott Street triangle. The government response was to open a children's prison (Loughan House in Co. Cavan), staffed by untrained prison officers. There was an outcry from all the childcare agencies. If the only response to the needs of inner city children was to lock them up as far away as possible, then the future of these children was very grim indeed, went the argument. The government took a hammering. And suddenly, here were three positive proposals landing on their desk. They jumped at the chance to be seen to be doing something more useful, and all three proposals were immediately accepted. Political opportunism saved the day, money no object. One hundred per cent funding for the residential hostel was guaranteed, in writing. Would we like a minibus between the three projects, they asked? No, we wanted a minibus each. We got a minibus each. For the first and only time in my life, I had a good relationship with the Eastern Health Board!

The hostel opened in 1979. It catered for six boys aged between twelve and sixteen, whose homes were so unsatisfactory that they deserved a better chance. It was a community-based hostel, catering for children from the local area and, as far as was possible, staffed by people from or with links to the local area and who knew the children well, before they even came near the hostel. It aimed to help young people cope, in a different and more positive way, with living in the community from which they came and in which they would probably remain for much of their lives. It was and continues to be reasonably successful.

However, after several years another problem became evident. When they reached the age of sixteen or seventeen, the young people were leaving the hostel and had nowhere to go except back to the streets or to the unsatisfactory homes they had left. The health boards only had responsibility for young people up to the age of sixteen. The local authority housing department only had responsibility for adults over eighteen (and with huge waiting lists for housing, it was an unfulfilled responsibility). Nobody had responsibility for young people between sixteen and eighteen. These youngsters were in a bureaucratic limbo – too old for child care and too young to be housed.

There was little point in running a hostel for young people if they were only going to return to the streets when they left. So we proposed opening a hostel for the sixteen to eighteen age-group as well. But we had no money and no house. I was living in Ballymun at this time, in a flat in a tower block. I asked Dublin Corporation for another flat in the block I was living in to house such a project and, to my surprise (and their regret ever since), they said yes.

So in 1983 we opened the flat and took in a few older homeless teenagers. I ran the flat on my own; if I was out, there was no staff or supervision. It would be irresponsible now, but at the time, it worked, to house such a project.

Next we applied for a grant to open a house, as the flat was hopelessly unsuited to providing a service to (sometimes difficult) homeless children. Again, Dublin Corporation came to the rescue, with capital funding. We opened the house in1985 but by that stage, so many young people were looking for accommodation that we were unable to close the flat. We had to run both, again with no money and no staff.

I applied everywhere for a grant to run the hostels. The Department of Justice wanted to know if the children were in trouble with the law; the answer was not all of them, so they didn't want to know. The Department of Education wanted to know if the children were in full-time education; the answer again was not all of them, so they didn't want to know. The Eastern Health Board wanted to know if the children were under sixteen; the answer was no, so they didn't want to know. The Department of Labour had absolutely no responsibility for homeless children, so they gave us £15,000 to pay a salary! We were delighted, we had a staff, although it consisted of only one person. He looked after the house; I looked after the flat.

In 1987 the National Lottery was set up. Here was an opportunity. Applications for funding were sent to all relevant departments. None wanted to know. However, I was friendly with the junior minister in the Department of Education and a phone call here and a word there and lo and behold, we got Lottery money. He hadn't even seen our application which was still sitting on a desk somewhere in the department. At last we could staff our hostels at least some of the time. We still had no money for food or clothes or outings or educational materials or anything else but we were glad to have staff and light and heat paid for by the Lottery.

So now we had two hostels, staff and some minimal security of funding. We still had to rely a lot on donations to pay our other bills.

But the numbers grew and grew. For years we had twelve children living in a three-bedroomed flat. On one famous night we had nineteen.

And the problems grew and grew too. Drugs became the major problem. Young people who were homeless, living a meaningless life, bored to tears on the street, feeling bad about themselves, depressed and wondering why God, if there is one, had bothered placing them on this earth, were being offered a few hours of escape, a bit of gear, an Ecstasy tab, a joint, which for a short time makes them feel good, gives them a buzz, and banishes the feelings of worthlessness and uselessness which they feel all the rest of the time. Who wouldn't take drugs if they were in that situation?

Later of course, when they discover what drugs are really all about, they want to get off them. They've had enough of the sickness, the dependency, the stealing. But there's the problem: they can't get off drugs while living on the street, and they can't get admission to a hostel while they are on drugs. So they're caught in a Catch-22 situation. We wanted to give young people a chance to get off drugs, so we took them in, even if they were on drugs, under certain conditions.

But then we had young people coming off drugs sleeping in the same room as young people doing their Leaving Certificates at school, and this was unhelpful, to say the least. So we opened another hostel, our 'quiet' house, for those who were crime-free, drug-free, alcohol-free and attending school or training courses. This worked well for a while, but then we ran out of 'quiet' lads!

That's the history of my life: nothing was ever planned; everything just happened. I worked with young people and saw some who were homeless, so I opened a hostel. By pure luck, it happened at the right time in the right place and money was made available. I saw young people leaving the hostel and going back on the streets, so I opened another hostel. The numbers grew and grew so I opened another hostel. The problems intensified, so I opened a 'quiet' house.

All the time, we never had enough money. As luck and God would have it, people sent donations without even being asked. We survived, thanks to them.

During all this time, I continued to change. I became more patient, coping with the personal difficulties that the young people presented. I became more accepting of what each day brought, the crises, the smaller problems, the good things that happened. My prayer deepened because I was so often praying the 'prayer of desperation' when confronted with seemingly insurmountable problems.

This 'prayer of desperation' taught me to face my own humanity and helplessness and let God be God. It is his Kingdom we are building, not our own. He knows what he is doing, he is still in charge, the Master Architect, I hope. It is his children who are dying, who are suffering and he has his reasons. I don't know what they are; if I did, I would be God.

My image of God changed. I had been brought up to see God as the one who loved each of us as individuals, equally. God had no favourites. His love was infinite and universal. And he asked us to love each other, as individuals, caring for those who crossed our path. All of that remains true, but I learned to see another side of God, as it were. I now have three images which describe the God in whom I believe.

The first encapsulates what I believe is most important to my God. This image is of parents watching their home burning down and their child is trapped on the top floor. What is in the parents' mind? What are they concerned about? Clearly they are not worried about the TV and video getting destroyed. They are not worried about whether or not they have sufficient insurance. Not that those things are unimportant. But at that moment they fade into insignificance. Their only concern, at that moment, is the safety of their child. And if a stranger should happen to pass by, what do they want from that person? Only that he or she would rescue their child. They are not worried about whether the stranger is divorced or not. They are not worried about whether his or her car is insured or not. Not that those things are unimportant. But at that moment they fade into insignificance. Rescuing their child becomes the priority beside which everything else becomes irrelevant.

I imagine God, the parent of all, looking down at this world, where so many suffer or are in danger. For God, everything fades into insignificance alongside the suffering of his children.

The second image reminds me that God has his favourites. This image is of a parent with two children. One is doing her homework and says to the parent: 'Can you help me with my homework?' The parent goes to help the child with her homework. If at that moment in time, the parent looks out the window and sees his other child being beaten up outside, what does he do? Well, obviously, he goes to the rescue of the child being beaten up. Why does he do so? He goes to the rescue of the child being beaten up, not because he loves that child more than the child doing the homework but because of the situation which the child is in. The child who is in danger, or suffering, has a priority call on the parent's care, concern and time which the other child, at least at that moment in time, does not have.

As my God looks down on this world, if he does not have a special care or concern for those who are suffering or in need, a concern and care which the rest of us do not require at least at this point in time, then God would not be a parent, but a monster.

The third image tells me what angers God. This image is of a man sitting at the side of a lake, enjoying the beautiful day, soaking up the sun, lazing the time away. There is a child paddling beside him in the lake. Suddenly, the child takes a step too far and is in out of his depth. He is splashing and shouting, looking for someone to rescue him. Imagine what the parents of that child would think if the fellow at the side of the lake did nothing to help the child. Wouldn't they be extremely angry? They would find it almost impossible to forgive him. Nothing that that man could have done to those parents could have been more offensive, more unforgiveable. Even if he had broken into their house in the middle of the night, stolen their TV and video and made off in their car and burnt it out, it would not have been as bad as what he actually did. And what did he do? He did absolutely nothing. He broke no law, broke no commandment. Yet his doing absolutely nothing when the child was in danger was the worst possible thing that man could have done to the parents. It would be different if he had fallen asleep and didn't hear the child or if he couldn't swim and was afraid of drowning himself. But if he just couldn't have been bothered to do anything to help the child, that would be unforgivable.

Those three images are an attempt to describe the God I pray to and the God whom I try to follow.

Now I see God as the parent of all of us, no matter who we are, or what group we belong to or what we may have done in the past. Every human being without exception has the dignity of being a child of God. Where that dignity is denied to anyone, where it is undermined by the way someone is treated in society, then God, as the parent of that person or that group of people, is being denied. And so my God asks me to protest, to protest in two ways, perhaps three ways.

Firstly, he asks me to affirm the dignity of that person or group through my own relationship with them, by reaching out to them in a preferential way and in that way, at least, affirming their dignity in the face of the contrary message they receive from society all the time.

Secondly, he asks me to protest publicly, in whatever way is open to me, as Jesus himself did, against the attitudes, policies and structures which deny people their dignity as children of the God we claim to worship and believe in.

Thirdly, he may ask me, as a consequence of those two actions, to become marginalised myself, through the opposition and attitudes of those who are offended or upset at the stands I take, and thereby begin to share in some small way the state of marginalisation of those whose dignity I am defending.

This willingness to enter into the life situation of those who are unwanted is to share, in some small way, the experience of the Son of God in his incarnation.

My God is on the side of those who are unwanted, uncared for, despised, rejected and marginalised. The idea that as a parent he is pained by their pain has become an integral and essential part of my understanding of God. I won't spend my life working with homeless children but I will want to spend the rest of my life affirming the dignity of those on the margins in whatever way my life, health, energy and provincial allow.

My God taught me not to plan too much. So many crises, so many unexpected events, good and bad, intervene in this work that my plans are often interrupted or even destroyed. I have learned to accept whatever comes, to hold plans very loosely. This has made me less rigid, less inflexible.

Why do I continue? many ask. Do you never feel like packing it in? It's like asking parents if they ever feel like packing it in. It is the relationship with the young people living with us that keeps me going. I know that I make a difference, at least to some, perhaps a great difference to a few. And I can't just walk away. Anyway, the job satisfaction is very good. I don't wake up in the morning wondering why I have to get up. Each day is a new wonder, a fresh excitement. If I can make a difference to even one person's life, then my own life has been worthwhile.

So where to now? I don't know. We have lived from hand to mouth all these years. We could run out of money any month now. I have learned not to hold my plans too rigidly. Anyway, I'm getting too old now to work with children. They no longer see me as a father figure, but as a grandfather figure. I'm losing my elasticity. I have less bounce. I'm more easily irritated. My life's work may very well change its direction, but not, I hope, its orientation. To walk away from those who are unwanted, to return to a safe and comfortable existence with those who are, fortunately, safe and comfortable, would be a denial of my God.

MOMENTS OF GRACE

Stanislaus Kennedy

I was born Treasa Kennedy during the Second World War on the Dingle Peninsula, between Holy Mount Brandon and the Atlantic Ocean. I was one of five children and my childhood was a traditional one, lived among fishermen and farmers, the caretakers of a peasant tradition. In my early childhood, there was story-telling and card-playing in place of radio, cinema, television. It was a life of mystery, beauty and simplicity. The pattern of the day, the night, the year, and even life itself was lived unself-consciously in the presence of God. The life of the people was deeply incarnational, whether saving the hay, telling the time from the sun and the tide, catching trout and salmon, going to stations, wakes, funerals, marriages, walking under hedges dripping with fuchsia – which we called 'deora Dé' (God's tears) – cutting and footing the turf or bringing tea to the fields or the bog. But it was not all joy. We also knew hardship through the Depression and the War, with its food rationing. Hard times drove many from their land. But we were a close and neighbourly community. As the local writer Peig Sayers (whom I knew) put it:

> We all helped each other, living in the shelter of each other. Everything that was coming dark upon us we would disclose. ... Friendship is the fast root in my heart; it is like a white rose in the wilderness.

I went to secondary school in Dingle, three miles away. Heading out the gate each day for school on my bike, the child was stealing out of me. It was a new world, dominated by nuns, where everything was correct and proper, and one was expected to be polite, in place and on time. I did well at school. I enjoyed the camaraderie of my friends, and I was often involved in mischief and escapades. But I was lonely at times too, lonely, unhappy, rebellious, moody.

As I grew up, I read that there were children who were neglected and poor in the bigger towns and cities, and I wanted to help them, but I didn't know how to go about it. (There were no training courses in social work in those days.) Then I heard of an order of nuns in Dublin who worked with the poor. I did not particularly want to be a nun, but it seemed to be the only way that I could work directly with the poor. That was how I stumbled upon the Sisters of Charity. What I didn't realise was that this was God's way of calling me to walk with him and with the poor.

A pre-Vatican II noviceship of rules, regulations, prayers and practices followed. It came as a shock to my youthful exuberance, but the companionship of the other novices, the deep spirituality of those who guided us, the serenity of some of the older sisters, the deep respect in which the sisters held the poor, and the idea that I would soon be working with the poor, in whom God resided in a special way, kept me going. Moments of grace.

After my noviceship, I went to work in a training school, laundry and youth club, at Stanhope Street Convent in Dublin, in the early 1960s. It was a new experience, sharing the hardship and humour of the poor of Dublin.

Then my life took an unexpected turn. A young bishop was appointed to the Diocese of Ossory, in Kilkenny. He was a man who had a great love for the poor, and he invited the Sisters of Charity to help him to establish social services in Kilkenny. This was the sort of work I was longing to do, but, as it happened, it wasn't I who made the decision. I was sent to join him. Moments of grace.

Bishop Birch was already being seen as different, a man ahead of his time. Treading new ground, he set out to build a domestic Church, where everyone was gift, bishop and clergy were servants of the people of God, and the poor and the marginalised were at the centre. Inspired by the bishop, it was the ideal for which I also worked, prayed, struggled and suffered for nearly two decades in Kilkenny, interrupted only by my undergraduate and postgraduate studies.

Together we were always discovering new ideas, new ways, new images, new visions, new needs, new services, new experiments. The young and the old, the rich and the poor, the able and the disabled, the sick and the well, the learned and the unlearned, the homed and the unhomed all had a place and a gift. Bringing the periphery into the centre, creating services, activities and communities, touching the hearts of the rich and poor alike, consoling the poor and disquieting the rich with the good news of the Gospel, we set out to build a new model of Church, vibrant, exciting, always changing, renewing, seeking, listening, searching, reading, waiting, speaking, campaigning, never satisfied. We invited new ideas, thoughts and people from all over the globe. Poets, artists, prophets and saints moved in and out of Kilkenny, many of them friends for life. Moments of grace.

National conferences on poverty and national programmes to combat poverty were all part of the 1970s. I was learning that we had to suffer with and for the poor. Living with insecurity and ambiguity, being understood and being misunderstood were part and parcel of living and working with the poor.

From Peter Birch's example, I learned to have a great sense of myself and a great sense of God. I learned to know where I began and where I left off, what area of myself I could yield to the encroachment of my enemies and what to the encroachment of those I loved. I learned to draw my inspiration from the Gospels and from my time alone, from nature and from music, literature and all forms of art, and from loving relationships with men and women.

Through Peter Birch, I met people I might never have met, dreamt dreams I might never have dreamt, and discovered gifts and talents in myself and others I might never have dared to. Above all I discovered the great gift and beauty those people who have been rejected by society can bring us if we can only stop and look, see and receive, and that the greatest temptation was not to look and see and act. Bishop Birch helped me to realise that what makes the Christian life worth living is a risky business, and that, despite the risks, we are all God's work of art. From him I learned that bit by bit, step by step, we become that work of art, if we allow our hearts to open and to unfold. Other seeds were being planted which would later come to fruition in me.

Bishop Birch's sudden and untimely death in 1981 came like a bolt from the blue. My soul was filled with a grief and a sorrow that I had never known before. His death seemed unbearable for a time. As well as a dear friend, I had lost the person who was the source of my inspiration. But sad though my loss was at the time, it was a beginning as well as an ending, the beginning of a new phase of my life. I had many friends to comfort me, but I knew I had to discover for myself where God was drawing me. Moments of grace.

Later that year, Jean Vanier, founder of L'Arche, whom I had met through Peter Birch some years earlier, came to visit, and with his visit the clouds began to lift. I had always been influenced by Jean's work and his commitment, but now he became my soul-guide and my inspiration. Living the Gospel in the L'Arche fraternity, committed totally to the restoration of a broken universe and acknowledging the special place of handicapped people in that restoration, he sustained, encouraged, inspired and guided me in the way of God's love, as my spiritual director and through the annual eight-day retreats that he led, to find my strength in my weaknesses in the bright and dark days and years of the 1980s and 1990s. Moments of grace.

I left Kilkenny and the people I loved for Dublin in 1983, in sadness and sorrow, but with trust in God, not knowing where I was being led or drawn. Attending the general chapter of the Sisters of Charity that summer opened new windows of hope. Reflecting on the spirit of Mary Aikenhead, founder of the

Religious Sisters of Charity, we challenged each other again to listen to the cry of the poor and break the walls of prejudice and fear that protect our security and limit our vision.

By October of that year I was a senior research fellow at University College Dublin, with eight research assistants, among them Rachel Collier. We set out, using a variety of research methods, to discover more about homeless women in Dublin – who they were, where they were, and what they thought about their situation. Rachel took the risk of forfeiting a promising career in journalism and voluntarily embarked on this mission without knowing where it would lead us, and still works closely with me. We discovered the hidden homeless – women who were without homes and hidden away – and we challenged the popular belief that there were few if any homeless women in Dublin.

Inspired by the women and with a donation of £5,000 from the Religious Sisters of Charity, Rachel and I rented the top floor of an inner-city building. We spent the following year with eight young women who had been homeless and whom we had met during the previous year's research. It was a year of exploring, examining, understanding and discovering the deeper meaning of being out of home. Eating, listening, reading, writing, crying and laughing, we shared our songs, poems, plays, joys and sorrows, hopes and fears, pains and struggles, the secrets of our souls. I came to realise in a deeper way that everyone who has been deeply hurt has the right to be sure that they are loved, that we all need a comforting presence to bring peace, hope and life, and that we all need and have a right to a place called home. During that year I learned in a very special way the wisdom of the excluded people, the rejected people, the women out of home, and I learned to let that wisdom guide me in a way I knew not. T.S. Eliot puts it this way in 'East Coker':

> In order to arrive at what you do not know
> You must go by a way which is the way of ignorance.
> In order to possess what you do not possess

You must go by the way of dispossession.
In order to arrive at what you are not
You must go through the way in which you are not.
And what you do not know is the only thing you know
And what you own is what you do not own
And where you are is where you are not.

I simply did not know where I was being led, but I knew deep in my heart that the wisdom of the spirit was speaking to me through these women, the rejected ones, and that wisdom continued to guide me in the years ahead. They knew the pain of powerlessness, homelessness, poverty and rejection. They knew what it was to be treated without dignity, respect or grace and they knew deep want and suffering caused by injustice, greed and power. They knew it in their minds and hearts, in their bodies and in their bones, in the deepest part of their being. But they also knew how things could be different.

During that year a new movement was being conceived, almost without our knowing it. As we set about identifying a name for the new organisation, I knew that I too needed a 'focus', a groundedness. And as we named the values that would underpin 'Focus Point', I too, with the women, named hospitality, safety, security, structure, compassion, equality, respect and dignity. We discovered how alike we all were in our common humanity, our giftedness, the frailty at the root of our creaturehood. That year had a profound effect on my life. I was helped to move into a sense of deep gratitude to and reverence for these women for all they taught me about myself, about humanity and about society, and gratitude to God for drawing me close to them and to him through them. As Jessica Powers puts it in her poem 'There is a Homelessness':

There is a homelessness, never to be clearly defined.
It is more than having no place of one's own, no bed or
    chair.

It is more than walking in a waste of wind,
or gleaning the crumbs where someone else has dined,
or taking a coin for food or clothes to wear.
The loan of things and the denial of things are possible to
  bear.

It is more, even, than homelessness of the heart,
of being always a stranger at love's side,
of creeping up to a door only to start,
at a shrill voice and to plunge back to the wide dark of one's
  own obscurity and hide.

It is the homelessness of the soul in the body sown;
it is the loneliness of mystery...

With six out of the original eight homeless women and the women who waked with them – two Marys, Kathleen, Michelle, Julie, Bernie, Colette, Carrie, Rosemary, Rachel and myself, later joined by Síle and Trish – Focus Point opened its doors and its heart to homeless people in September 1985, providing the services identified by homeless women during the previous two years. We were bringing dignity onto the street.

Focus Point's work grew and extended, and in time we complemented our work in crisis services by providing good-quality housing for vulnerable people who otherwise could not afford it. Stanhope Street Convent, where I was first missioned in the early 1960s, was to become the site of our first housing project, made possible by the donation of the convent building by the Sisters of Charity; and the Presentation and Holy Faith Sisters have since made property available to us for housing for people who would otherwise be unhoused. The Focus work has continued to expand and develop over the years, and by 1994 we were starting to move outside Dublin to help local communities working to provide supportive housing for people with housing needs in provincial towns and cities.

Focus is a story about people, wonderful people, giving and receiving. It is the story of bringing into the light the hidden lives of many. It is a story of adventure, risk, dynamic activity and self-giving. It is a story about development and growth, having grown to its present size with over seventy staff and as many volunteers, twelve different projects, providing housing for over three hundred people in Dublin alone, with plans for two hundred more apartments outside Dublin, and ministering to over three thousand homeless men, women, young people and children in crisis every year. Services, activities, houses, communities, self-help, giving, receiving, research, publications, protests, marches, campaigns, celebrations, reflection, miracles, joy and laughter are all part of life at Focus Point Ireland (as the organisation is now called). It brings hope, life, love, safety, respect, structure, security, rights and dignity into all our lives. Moments of grace.

But it is also a story of suffering, sickness, struggle, injustice, oppression, being let down, being put down. When things were going well, I rejoiced, and when things weren't going so well, I often felt deflated, and then I sat and wept. Then came change – an inspiration, a prayer, a rest, a word, a friend, prayer, reflection, a sabbatical, a retreat – and winter changed to spring, forces awakened, life seemed to surge once more, with the unswerving certainty that I should go on with determination and joy. I knew that I carried within me all the weakness and frailties of all humankind as well as all the possibilities for growth and development.

Through all this, I learned about my own vulnerability and human frailty. I have learned that these human frailties, which I fear, and which I try to run from, to wipe out, to cover up, are my saving grace. These human frailties that have humbled and at times even humiliated me have also held me up and reminded me again and again that I have absolutely no right to point the finger at any human being. It is precisely these frailties that led me and drew me to walk with God and with the poor.

Each day I become more aware that I am not complete, not

finished, not self-sustaining, not self-ensuring. This knowledge can make one fearful and guarded, but I know it can force me to make room and space in my heart for God's love and grace and the gift of my brothers and sisters, especially those who are most excluded. I have learned that my fullest solidarity with the poor only comes about to the degree to which I am willing to enter into the mystery of my own frail, fragile and at times uncontrollable humanity. It is the neediness and poverty of my humanity that ties me to all humanity and that brings me the gifts of faith, hope and love. It is when I am most secure, most strong, most powerful, most in control, that I am most weak and empty and it is when I am weak that I am strong.

There came a point, in the 1990s, when Focus Point Ireland was alive, strong and healthy, and I knew it. It could and would continue well without me at the helm. And so I made way for others to take over, realising that it was time for me to be with the organisation in a new way. That small voice within reminded me that I was now into my fifties, and the time had come to search anew and find a new way to be present to the poor. I still carried within me the seeds of contemplation, waiting to be nurtured, wounds waiting to be healed, rocks waiting to be moved, a body awaiting rest, ideas waiting to be realised, gifts waiting to be claimed and reclaimed, the mystic and artist waiting to be matured, God's work of art awaiting a different kind of stroke. I stand again with myself and my God, to learn afresh where I am being drawn, with the same faith and trust with which I left the Dingle Peninsula for Dublin, Dublin for Kilkenny, and Kilkenny for Dublin again, believing, like Adrienne Rich, that

> Our gifts compel
> master our ways and lead us in the end
> To where we are most ourselves.

Moments of grace and miracles.

JOURNEY WITH THE POOR

Edward J. Farrell

In 1931, the third year of the Depression, I was born in a workers' neighbourhood in Detroit, Michigan. Looking west from my bedroom window, I could see the 'Eight Sisters', the tall chimney stacks of the Ford Rouge factory a mile away. Each day I could see the factory workers on the always crowded Baker streetcar, an electric trolley, rumbling and swaying down Vernor Highway to the end of the line at the Rouge Plant. Ninety-five thousand men worked on the assembly line, turning out six thousand cars a day. Today the same assembly line produces more cars with one-tenth of the workers. In 1937 Walter Ruether began to organise the union, and stories circulated in the neighbourhood about the 'goon' squads that raided homes in the neighbourhood and beat those who signed up for the union. I overheard the hushed conversations of men gathered in small groups and felt a sense of powerlessness and fear. My father was laid off from his job as a body-finisher and car trimmer at the Fisher body plant. For several years he was an orderly at Ford Hospital. I would go with him on his day off to collect his weekly cheque. We would take the streetcar through the African-American neighbourhood ghettos. When I asked, I was told that these were the 'poor people'.

In 1938, while riding with my mother on a streetcar heading into downtown Detroit, we passed The Catholic Workers' St Francis House of Hospitality with a long, long line of men waiting outside. 'Who are those people?' I asked. My mother told me that it was the 'bread line', for people who had nothing to eat because there was no work for them. I have a vague memory of walking to the city dump, a land-fill for a future park. I saw people living in shacks and I saw them picking through the dump for food and salvageable materials. My father, to the consternation of my mother, would often bring home a stranger he had met on the avenues for my mother to feed.

As a twelve-year-old paper boy, I canvassed many neighbourhoods door-to-door. I was welcomed into many homes. It was always in the poorer neighbourhoods that I was welcomed and that people would sign up for a subscription to the paper. I discovered that even though they had less, they were more generous – maybe that is why they were poor.

In the seminary high school I met Jimmy Hoepwell, the first African-American person I would know as a friend. He was the only African-American person in a school of four hundred students. I worked with him in the Blessed Martin League which went to various high schools to try to involve students in the social issues of our inner city. In 1943 there had been a so-called race riot at Belle Isle, our largest city park, an island in the Detroit River. The fall-out fear triggered the panic move to the suburbs to put distance between the poorer 'Blacks' and the more affluent 'Whites'.

Later in high school I discovered the Detroit Catholic Worker. I would go with other seminarians to downtown Detroit and work on the bread line and then sit around and listen to their stories. Dorothy Day 'on pilgrimage' would visit the Detroit Catholic Worker and stay at Martha House, the home of Lou and Justine Murphy. Lou and Justine were cornerstone people in my life. Soon after they graduated from college and married, they were drawn into the Catholic Worker Movement and made a life commitment to voluntary poverty, personal responsibility for society, and the corporal and spiritual works of mercy. They were the Gospel made visible. In the midst of the poor of the city, they raised their eight children. Each person in need was welcomed into their home. They accepted each one as an 'ambassador for Christ'. What I was being taught in the seminary, they made visible and tangible in their lives.

Fr Clement Kern, who was pastor of Holy Trinity Parish in

downtown Detroit, was known as 'the skid-row priest'. He was assigned in 1943 to this poor parish to phase it out and it was still blooming when he died in 1986. *Time* magazine was to describe him as 'the greatest little priest in America'. There was no intern deaconate programme in the fifties, but another seminarian and I wanted to get some experience of parish ministry before our ordination, so we went to see Fr Kern, and he invited us to live with him for part of the summer. He suggested that we do a census of the skid-row flop-houses, where the alcoholics and the destitute were housed. Many died there, alone and nameless. Fr Kern hoped that we could find a contact person in each flop-house who would know of Trinity parish and who could refer people to the parish, especially those who were dying. We spent a whole month visiting thirty-eight flop-houses, talking to whoever would talk to us. We established contact with twenty-two 'in charge' men who promised to come to a meeting at Holy Trinity church. What excitement we felt on the evening of our first organisational meeting. Refreshments were set up and everything was arranged. We were full of anticipation, but nobody showed up, not even one person. No one even telephoned. Fr Clem simply said, 'Anything worth doing is worth doing even though nothing seems to come of it'.

In my first parish assignment after ordination, a large Christian family movement (CFM) developed. Married couples met every two weeks to observe, judge, and act in their families, neighbourhoods and communities. They reflected upon scripture and liturgy and applied it to their lives. This was the beginning of small Christian communities within the parish. It helped the participants to develop a social conscience and an awareness of their responsibility as Christians to become involved beyond their immediate families. The CFM was a conscience-raising experience. People began to see that each family could do something for others. Fr James Keller's words, 'You can change the world', echoed in the background of their efforts. Families developed a perspective and a generosity that changed their traditional lifestyle. City-wide meetings at the University of Detroit, a local Catholic college, and national conferences at Notre Dame University opened up a new vision and new hopes.

This first parish to which I was assigned was located in an exclusively white suburban area. As an outreach, CFM members linked with St Agnes Parish in the inner city of Detroit. Our objective was to meet African-Americans and to make friends through shared experiences. It was a culture shock for many. Racism was such a dark part of our lives. African-Americans were almost always in lesser work roles. The two groups of Catholics seemed to have nothing in common until they sat down and shared their lives as couples and parents, and through this interchange discovered a common human bond.

From my parish work I became aware of many divorced women who had chosen not to remarry and who had children to support. In the 1950s and 1960s there was little parish support for Catholic divorcees. They did not fit into any parish organisation, but there was a society for single working women called St Martha's Guild. They met once a month at a convent for the cloistered sisters of Mary Reparatrix, whose ministry included sponsoring retreats for women in the Detroit archdiocese. There was much hesitancy about hosting a retreat for divorced Catholic women, but they finally agreed, and the first retreat for these women was held in 1964. From this retreat, attended by over thirty women, Bethany, an association for Catholic divorcees, emerged. Monthly meetings were held at the convent of the Dominican Sisters of the Sick Poor and other localities. These meetings consisted of a 'holy hour' before the Blessed Sacrament, followed by sharing. Soon there were four regions with monthly meetings in each location. Many of these women were forced into involuntary poverty, but by coming together they became life-givers to themselves and to each other.

Another organisation that began in the early 1960s in Detroit, the automotive capital of the world at that time, was the Detroit Industrial Mission (DIM). It was an ecumenical ministry to the automotive industry, which included the 'Big Three', Ford, Chrysler and General Motors. Protestant ministers and Catholic priests offered seminars and workshops that encouraged workers to reflect on and act on the Gospel in their workplace. Two of the ministers worked on the assembly line for several years and were active in the unions. Others worked in the area of management and offered consultation and symposiums. I worked at Ford in the engineering building, where there were ten thousand engineers. We led a programme called 'Freedom and Decisions'. The purpose was to reflect on how our particular work and Ford affected the neighbourhood, the city, the country and the world. Ford had thousands of personnel all over the world and had a major impact on people's lives worldwide. We asked ourselves, 'How do I influence world policy and decisions?' and believed that if we were not part of the vision and solution then we were 'the problem'. Without a vision of responsibility, the whole country becomes poor.

In the 1960s, when I was appointed to the Sacred Heart Seminary, the area surrounding the seminary had become totally occupied by African-Americans. During one summer I was drawn to live in an apartment building geographically located in St Agnes Parish. There were 102 units. All the residents of the building were black. I soon came to know more people in the apartment building than did the management. Hardly anyone knew their next-door neighbours. It was too risky. Each one lived in total anonymity. I would go from door to door introducing myself. I let them know I was living there and would like to come to know them. I was wearing my Roman collar, but that meant nothing to most of them. My presence generated a great deal of suspicion. I was thought to be a policeman in disguise or someone from the welfare department. Few invited me into their apartment, but I invited them to mine. I made a few friends who still remain in contact with me after thirty years. I arranged an open house afternoon at the nearby church of St Agnes, and delivered a personal invitation to each one. No one showed up on that Sunday afternoon. After six weeks I knew I could live my whole life in Apartment 102 and make no difference at all. Years later, when I became pastor of St Agnes Parish, I was surprised at the people who would come to me because they knew that I had lived in one of the apartment buildings in their area that summer, some fourteen years earlier. The poor do not forget the smallest kindness.

In 1966 I made the first retreat Jean Vanier gave, near Toronto in Canada. I was surprised to see mentally handicapped people making the retreat. These 'poor' people revealed to me my own poverty. I did not know how to relate to them. I did not know how to simply be with them and not 'do' anything that would make me more comfortable. How strange it was for me to be ministered to by people with disabilities. As someone was to tell me later, 'Don't talk. Don't hurry.' It was so hard for me not to be 'helpful'. It was so hard to learn that I could be most helpful by doing nothing, by simply being present, by wasting time in order to let others know that they were worth my time and I was worth theirs.

As pastor of an inner city 'poor' parish – poor economically, but rich in personality and family – I spent twelve years with what society calls 'the poor'. There were twenty thousand people in one square mile; one per cent, or two hundred, were Catholic. We ministered to six hundred people who were not Catholic but who were drawn to our parish through many different programmes.

I feel poor because I can do so little. How I wish I could change something of the welfare system! Easy fantasy is an escape from reaching out to one person. Yet one person does make a difference even if it is just for the individual who is touched by his or her efforts. One woman, Sr Leila, a Sister of Mercy, volunteered to work at St Agnes Parish while I was pastor. She had retired by then, but she had been administrator of Mount Carmel, an 800-bed hospital in inner-city Detroit. Her ministry in the parish was simply to take the mentally handicapped people who lived in adult foster care homes in the parish to lunch on a one-to-one basis. Most had never been taken out to lunch in their entire lives. Someone once said to Mother Teresa, 'Your work is only a drop in the ocean.' Her response was 'One drop changes the whole ocean.'

So many disturbing memories from my retreats, especially to developing world countries, linger in me and haunt me. As a student in Rome in 1953, I remember the people who were living in the walls of the city, people who were homeless, workless and family-less. My visit to India in 1969, when I saw streets filled with destitute sick and maimed, is embedded in my memory. I was overwhelmed by the numbers of men, women and children who lived in a constant state of near-starvation. The smell of death was everywhere. In Recife, La Paz, Lima and Belize I could not get away from the noise or the crush of the crowds. There was no privacy, no silence, no space. In Soweto, Haiti and Mexico City the unfathomable effects of economic and racial oppression, which cause enormous disparity and unbelievable inequality, continue to haunt me. Even in Jerusalem the hatred, mistrust and disproportionate advantages and opportunities given to one group as opposed to another crushed me. Immense gaps between people exist worldwide. Such disproportionate inequity touches every sphere of human existence: the economic, the educational, the psychological and the cultural. Life is not fair.

The experience of the poor has confronted me with my own poverty. I am poor because I have never had the genius to make a significant difference for people in need. I am poor because I have done so little. I am poor because I live so comfortably. The Gospel is a constant reminder to me that I must live an option for the poor, that I must be in solidarity with the poor, that the poor will set me free. The poor are a constant reminder to me that I must resist affluence. As Fr Hessler says, 'Make friends with the poor; they will be our judges.'

Who are the poor? What are my images of the poor? How do I 'feel' about the poor? There are so many who are truly poor.

There are those who are poor in their capacity to relate to others because they have spent their lives unloved. They have always been treated with anger, with rejection, with insensitivity. No one has ever truly cared for them. There are the poor who are depressed, who have no joy, no 'wine', nowhere to lay their heads, no-one to rely on, nowhere they can find true comfort for the sorrows that rack their souls. The poor are those who cannot care for themselves because of physical, emotional or mental disabilities. The poor are those who are chronically sick or chronically unhappy. The poor are those who are educationally retarded, culturally amoral, politically immoral, or spiritually anorexic. There are poor in every social stratum of society. Sometimes the poorest among us are those who do not even recognise our own poverty.

Even as a child, I felt a deep ache about inequality and poverty, about life and tragedy. I am so aware of the crises and disasters which affect ordinary people and disrupt the life of good people: natural disasters, national disasters and family disasters. Everything is so fragile, so close to absurdity and meaninglessness. I fall easily into the despair of history, into the mystery of evil. I cry out to the heavens, 'Why!', 'How long, O Lord!' I find myself plunged back into the Lamentations of Jeremiah – a form of prayer that I never knew of myself but which is born out of our contemporary world. I hear again Solzhenitsyn's prayer when he arrived in Magadan, Siberia, his first stop on his return to Russia after twenty years of exile in America. Magadan was the port through which passed upwards of three million political prisoners who were worked, beaten or frozen to death in Siberia under Stalin. Solzhenitsyn prayed that this land which has been hallowed by the death of so many innocent lives would be a light for all of Russia. Since that time he has gone from city to city proclaiming repentance.

The mystery of the crucifixion touches me in the lives of so many. I think of Paul Williams, a parishioner of St Agnes, who received a kidney transplant from his brother, but the medication he had to take led to the partial amputation of his hands and feet. He is my stigmatist. I am tempted to run away not only from my own pain but to escape the untold, obvious pain of other lives. At times I ask myself: 'How do I escape? How can I forget and erase what I know, what I have seen, what I have encountered?' I attempt to flee into amnesia, into inertia, into judgment and condemnation, into moralising, into television, into my own little world and cry out, 'I don't or can't care.' I make the world the size of my own family and my circle of friends. I make the world the size of my own needs, wants, perspectives and comfort. I am overwhelmed. I ask, 'What can I do about it?' 'Can I do anything?' 'Will anything I do make a difference?' 'Is it all a game?' 'Am I an actor on a stage? Can I not play any role I want?'

What overwhelms me is not just the simple facts but that so few seem to *care*. I am astonished when I hear good Christians say 'They are not my responsibility', 'It is none of my business', 'This is the way life is', 'You accept and live with it', 'The poor you will always have with you.' I am coming to understand that the 'poor' are the physically and spiritually numb, the well-off and talented people who have lost their capacity for compassion, who do not see, hear, or feel – whose very possessions and talents have so absorbed and diminished their humanity that they cannot experience anyone outside their immediate family. The very gifts that have been given in order to redistribute the pain, abandonment and rejection have become the means of flight and have created tombs of self-enclosure to seal themselves off from the 'others'. If our love of compassion is not developed we lose the capacity to love ourselves and we have to 'love' things that cannot respond to love – and the human heart dies.

I become more and more conscious of the cultural slogans which bombard us: 'Be happy any way you want', 'Enjoy yourself', 'Do it', 'Who cares?' 'Make your own bubble', 'Take care of Number One', 'Live as comfortably as you can', 'Why bother? Be carefree'. I am tempted to be a spectator, an observer of life and of others. If I allow myself to be a companion of the poor, if they give me their permission to walk with them, then I am constantly forced to ask myself these questions: What can I do without? What can I give away? What time and energy do I make available for others? When have I been extravagant? Foolish? With whom do I make friends? Those who are only like myself or those who are different from me? Those who have not had the opportunities and advantages I have been given? Whom do I invite to my table? Those who can invite me back? Or do I go out into the streets and bring in the poor, the lame, the blind, the homeless, the 'lepers' of our society, those who have no ability to return the favour to me? Why do I avoid the poor? What can I do in response for all that has been given to me? Why do I know so much and do so little?

All my life I have been disturbed and made uncomfortable by Jesus' command, 'If you want to be my disciple, sell all that you have, give it to the poor and come follow me.' I still hear the public confession of Fr Frank Norris, who gave one of my first retreats, 'I am not free to preach the Gospel, for I am not poor.' I am so indebted to those whom the media call 'poor'. How they have shaped and formed my life! How they have ministered to me and given me themselves, their friendship, their wisdom and courage! How poor a disciple I have been of theirs! How I have been evangelised and drawn into the Gospel! How I have been embarrassed by their generosity! Hattie McAllen, a welfare widow, gave me a polaroid camera my first Christmas at St Agnes. I had to be careful when I visited their homes. If I admired something, they wanted to give it to me. The advantage of being poor in possession compels one to develop every survival gift in oneself. 'Blessed are those who have no option but are driven into their deepest and most authentic self.' Yet how many others are driven to violence or madness! I am no longer astonished by the violence or the insanity but I continue to be astonished and humbled by the joy, peace and forgiveness that breaks through again and again.

I experience hope when I hear that a Presbyterian

congregation in the north-eastern suburbs of a Detroit community has committed itself to tithe fifty per cent of its income to an option for the poor. If the Christian churches in this country ever dared to tithe twenty per cent of their income to housing, health and education, no one would be forced to live below the poverty line. Just on the material level, seventy per cent of our people live more comfortably because thirty per cent are compelled to live as Aristotle says 'under the table' rather than around our table of abundance.

Affluence, individualism, 'comfort-zone spirituality' have numbed the vision of the common good. So many things, so much media, absorb most of our energy and time. I wonder if a revolution is smouldering beneath the surface. How long will it take for the Berlin Wall of the suburban churches to be dismantled? Will the breath of the third millennium, already hovering over this last decade of the twentieth century, release a hidden unveiled compassion? Will the Gospel be rediscovered? Will Paul's words in Ephesians 4: 17-24 ignite our post-Vatican II world?

> In particular I want to urge you in the name of the Lord, not to go on living the aimless kind of life that pagans live. Intellectually they are in the dark, and they are estranged from the life of God, without knowledge, because they have shut their hearts to it. Their sense of right and wrong once dulled, they have abandoned themselves to sexuality and eagerly pursue a career of indecency of every kind. Now that is hardly the way you have learnt from Christ, unless you failed to hear him properly when you were taught what the truth is in Jesus. You must give up your old way of life; you must put aside your old self, which gets corrupted by following illusory desires. Your mind must be renewed by a spiritual revolution so that you can put on the new self that has been created in God's way, in the goodness and holiness of the truth.

I am so encouraged by book like *Common Fire – Lives of Commitment In A Complex World*, a sequel to Robert Bellah's *Habits of the Heart*. The four authors, Laurent and Sharon Parks-Daloz and Cheryl and James Keen, interviewed and studied more than a hundred people in many walks of life who live and work on behalf of the common good. This landmark book documents so clearly that the person-to-person, interpersonal perspective, is no longer adequate. *Systemic thought and collaboration* is crucial to managing the 'complexity of urban conflict, polarising economy and environmental degradation' – a complex description of our brothers and sisters in need. Person-to-person, immediate help is always necessary but it is not enough. The person-to-person approach is limited and often distorted in the absence of a larger, systematic perspective. Seeing whole, one can recognise how the economic system makes welfare inevitable by creating a permanent underclass. Systems shape behaviour in ways that may be invisible from an interpersonal perspective. By viewing problems as systemic in nature, we can conceive solutions that go beyond mere exhortations for individuals to work harder.

Where do we find people who can shun cynicism and despair, accept new responsibilities, build new connections and sustain themselves over the long haul? What goes into the formation and development of this 'new breed'? *Common Fire* focuses on seven components:

1. Connection and Complexity – The Challenge of the New Commons
2. Community – Becoming at Home in the World
3. Compassion – Living Within and Beyond Tribe
4. Conviction – Developing Critical Habits of Mind
5. Courage – A Responsible Imagination
6. Confession – The Struggle with Fallibility
7. Commitment – The Power of the Double Negative

Professor Carlyle of Harvard is quoted: 'Malcom X was always trying to change individuals; Martin Luther King, Jr was trying to change society. You have to do both if you want real progress. It's important to change an individual who thinks there is no hope, and it's important to change the system that destroys hope. You have to do both... You can only help people with people.'

I remember walking with Martin Luther King Jr in 1965 in Grosse Pointe, an affluent suburb of Detroit, facing a barrage of hate and venom, being spat upon, and called 'Judas!' by Sunday Christians. King not only told the poor that they count, but count most profoundly because we hold clues to the soul of America, to redeeming the soul of America. That was thirty years ago.

Common Fire concludes with four primary directions:

1. Create time to pause, reflect, assess.
2. Cultivate the strengths of living both within and beyond the tribe.
3. Develop and practise a consciousness of connection.
4. Attend to the character and use of language.

The epilogue focuses on twelve sectors of our society, each representing a critical feature of our common life, a particular set of perspectives, responsibilities and opportunities. Each sector can make a strategic contribution to the formation of a shared moral compass, helping us to get our bearing as we work together to create a positive future. The sectors are: household (children, family, youth); schools; higher education; professions and professional education; religion; arts and media; public policy; business; non-profit organisations; the health and therapeutic community; foundations and philanthropies and the reader.

'Indira Web', a central image in Hinduism, suggests that the ultimate reality, the universe, is a web in which each node is a living being. Each one is influenced by everything else in the universe. Frederick Bnechnor reflects: 'The place God calls you is the place where your deep gladness and the world's deep hunger meet.' Someone else added, 'It's not that I sustain a commitment but I am sustained by the commitment that it is continually reborn in that place.'

All of this led me to announce, on 21 August 1992, a national network called *The Friends of the Poor* at the Sixth Academy for Spiritual Formation in Sumatanga, Alabama. The following is the prelude to this national network:

'As you sent me into the world, I have sent them into the world… May these be completely one that the world will realise that it was you who sent me and you have loved them as much as you loved me.' (John 17:18, 23)

Our twentieth century has been called the century of world violence. One hundred and twenty-five million people died violently in the first two-thirds of the century. Out of this terrible carnage and suffering, a new level of higher consciousness and deeper prayer has welled up in ordinary people around the world. So much so that the last third of the twentieth century will mark our times as the century of a new, yet ordinary, spirituality and contemplation, one that leads to compassion and presence to the poor.

Traditionally, spirituality and contemplation have been for monasteries and convents, for monks and nuns. Yet Jesus was not a monk, he never lived in a monastery. He chose to live in the midst of people. Jesus was and is a contemplative in the midst of the poor. He wept over his city. He wept with those who grieved. He said, 'Where I am, I want you to be'. In the poor are our greatest riches, our deepest truth. In and with the poor, we will discover how poor we are and, in that truth, we will discover freedom.

Every city is a holy city. Every city continues to be Bethlehem, Nazareth, Jerusalem. A city is holy because God dwells among the people there and is waiting for us to meet him where he had gone ahead of us. In our contemplation, we will recognise God living, loving, suffering, dying and rising. We are called to live in the heart of the city in the heart of God because this is God's dwelling place. Where God is, God wants us to be.

Elijah once complained to Yahweh that there wasn't one person in all Israel who remained faithful. And Yahweh had to reveal to the great prophet that God had kept seven thousand true to his name. I am beginning to think that we may be in a new age of Elijah. I am convinced that the Lord always keeps seven thousand true in every metropolitan area, even if the prophets do not recognise them. Jewish tradition carries the story of the 'lamed vow', the thirty-six just people who held the world together by their prayer, suffering and love – even if they do not recognise themselves. Our world continues to be held together by those seven thousand – or those thirty-six or some other number – by their faith, hope and love.

How good it would be to have a network of the people who recognise that God has made a covenant of friendship with them for the poor, people drawn so deeply into contemplation they are compelled to go and discover and share the hidden Christ in the broken and marginal of our world.

And so I announced a network: *The Friends of the Poor*. It is there. It is reality. I did not start it. I merely named it. It is a reality that I recognise. If you are a member, you will immediately recognise it as well.

THE SAINT AND THE SONG OF SIXPENCE

Tim Kearney

> O Angel of God
> my guardian dear,
> to whom God's love
> commits me here,
> ever this day and ever this night
> be at my side,
> to light, to guard,
> to rule and guide.
> Amen.

My spiritual journey began with these words. I was a little boy preparing for sleep. I was aware of my mother sitting on my bed beside me. She made me feel safe, and no matter how tired or restless I might feel at the end of the day, I became calm and still because she was there. Night-prayers always ended with the same poetry of words. More important than the words, however, was the presence of the one who spoke them. This was where my intuition was formed that if God was a father, then he must have the heart of a mother.

I was born into a middle-class Catholic family in Cork city in the late 1950s, one of seven children. Childhood years were marked by my sense of belonging to a warm and loving family which, like any other family, also had its fragilities and dysfunctions. My parents were well-off, but they did not believe in hoarding their money. They preferred to spend it on their children, providing us with a good education, wonderful summer holidays by the sea in West Cork and a deep-seated appreciation of the good things of life, as experienced most directly in my mother's cooking. Looking back on my childhood years, I am reminded of Hilaire Belloc's lines:

Wherever a Catholic sun doth shine,
There's plenty of laughter and good red wine!

I went to primary school with the Christian Brothers in Cork, and to secondary school as a boarder with the Irish Benedictines in Glenstal Abbey in Co. Limerick.

After leaving school I took a year out and worked as a volunteer with the Race Relations Commission in England, working mainly with West Indian and Asian minorities. I returned to Ireland to study at University College Dublin, when, out of the blue, an important turning-point in my life occurred. Jean Vanier, the founder of L'Arche, was giving one of his retreats in Dublin. My brother Richard and I had travelled up from Cork that weekend to attend the Dublin Theatre Festival. Neither of us, I must confess, was very interested in prayer, community life, the handicapped or retreats at that time. When another brother, Michael, invited us both along to listen to Jean Vanier give the introductory talk of his retreat that Sunday night, we agreed reluctantly, as the theatre festival was not starting until the following night.

However, we were not disappointed. For me it was quite an extraordinary encounter. I remember he began by quoting the words of Stephen Verney, an Anglican Bishop from the UK: 'We are more earthly and more heavenly than we can ever imagine.' What touched me most that night was the way in which Jean embodied his radical Gospel vision in his own person. There was a joy, a serenity and an inner freedom that radiated through his whole person, in his face and in his hands. He was not just preaching an inspiring Christian vision, but he was living it in his own life. I was touched by the authenticity of his life and by his uncompromising commitment to Jesus and to people with disabilities, with whom he shared his life in community in a personal way.

His words stirred the presence of my spirit within me that night, and planted a seed in the soil of my inner self. It was for me a turning-point in my spiritual journey. It came at a point in my life when I carried a good deal of inner anger, confusion and hurt with regard to the question of God, in general, and the institutional Church, in particular. But now I could assent to the notion of a God who chose to dwell not so much in laws and institutions but in the brokenness and beauty of the human heart. I could say yes to a God who chose not to impose himself upon me from outside, but to touch me from within, a God who was not impregnable but vulnerable and who identified in a special way with the poor and the handicapped, in whom he was present in a discreet but very real way.

My brother Richard was also deeply touched and impressed by Jean Vanier's words that night, to the extent that he decided, along with me, to attend the rest of the retreat, even though it meant missing most of the theatre festival. For two such lovers of theatre and the arts, that was quite a strong tribute to the inspiration and charisma of the founder of L'Arche.

This significant experience was followed by six years of undergraduate and postgraduate study of philosophy, history and literature in UCD, during which time the seed that was planted at Jean Vanier's retreat began to be nurtured and to grow.

When we take a leap of faith, and we embark on a spiritual journey and commit ourselves to developing a personal relationship with God, it is quite amazing how God sends us certain people on our way to challenge, sustain and nourish us. During my years of study and teaching at UCD, two such individuals were to have an important impact on my evolving spiritual journey.

The first was Michael Paul Gallagher SJ, the charismatic and popular lecturer in English literature in UCD, who was my teacher and who became my friend and my spiritual guide. He invited my brother Philip and me to set up a prayer group with him on campus, which we did and which soon became an inclusive and nourishing resource for many young students who were seeking support in their inner journey and in the ways of prayer and of the heart. Michael Paul often used to tell me the three groups of people he most admired were 'poets, madmen and saints, for they were the most authentic seekers of truth, and the wisest keepers of the mystery and meaning of life'. His thinking was an important influence on my own spirituality and vision.

The second influence was an extraordinary woman called Ann Eastwood. Though diminutive in stature, she was large in personality and wise in the ways of the Spirit. Ann had two houses north of the Liffey which she let out as flats. My brother Philip and I went to stay in a flat in the house in which Ann lived for an interim two-week period, while we searched for a more suitable location close to the university on the south side of Dublin. Our searching, however, came to naught and we ended up spending the next five years living with Ann, who soon became not just our landlady but our friend and sister in community as well.

By the end of that first year, we were living as a small Christian community, sharing our evening meal and a time of prayer each night. Through our sharing of daily life together in community we soon got to know each other, warts and all. So as well as eating and praying together, we also began to get on each other's nerves and to have our arguments. We began to discover the reality of community life both in its richness and in its demands. Forgiveness and reconciliation and the ability to celebrate and to have a laugh were at the heart of it all.

Ann was a wonderful teacher in the ways of community. She was also a woman of prayer. She didn't talk about prayer very much, or spiritualise about it; she just did it and got on with it in such a way that we could see it was at the centre of her life, the still point of her turning world, her source of energy and of inspiration. Every morning she would spend two hours of prayer in the Blessed Sacrament Chapel, which was then in D'Olier Street. I always had the feeling about Ann that she had access to a mysterious inner spirit and strength which had the power to move mountains. It was thanks to Ann Eastwood that the Little Sisters of Jesus first came to Ireland in the 1970s, when she made one of her properties available to them. It was also thanks to Ann that my brother Philip (who is today ministering as a priest in a L'Arche community in France) and I were able to foster our growing relationship with Jean Vanier, as Jean would always come to stay with Ann whenever he visited Ireland, which was at least once a year.

Towards the end of my time in UCD, I did two years of postgraduate study on the poetry and philosophy of W.B. Yeats, and I lectured part-time in the Anglo-Irish Department of UCD and in All Hallows College. I was fascinated by Yeats' lifelong personal quest for what he termed 'unity of being', a condition which he embodied in some of his most inspired and memorable images:

> O body swayed to music,
> O brightening glance,
> How can we tell the dancer
> From the dance?

Much of the creative tension of his poetry comes from his own inner struggle to find this wholeness and unity not just in his art but in his life. As he put it in one of his lesser known poems, 'The Choice':

> The intellect of man is forced to choose,
> perfection of the life, or of the work.

Yeats was haunted by this dilemma throughout his life, but in one of the last letters he ever wrote to a close friend of his, he said:

> When I try to put all into a phrase, I say, man can embody truth, but he cannot know it.... You can refute Hegel, but not the saint nor the song of sixpence.

The song of sixpence was William Blake's symbol for the small joys and epiphanies hidden in the everyday things of life as well as a symbol of art. Unity of being might not be easily defined in rational philosophical terms (Hegel), but it could be captured intuitively both in the story of the saint and in the song of sixpence.

Yeats' quest and struggle for 'unity of being' mirrored my own personal search for meaning, and for a life choice that would in some way nourish my own inner seeking. I had my own dilemma to resolve. My professor, Gus Martin, was encouraging me to apply for a full-time lecturing post that was coming up in the department, while at the same time, Jean Vanier had invited me to take a year out after my MA to live in his L'Arche community in France. Though I loved the academic life with its study and teaching, and though I was being spiritually nourished in my involvement with campus ministry, there was still an emptiness within me which was not being filled. I didn't want to burn my bridges and possibly lose the chance of a secure and interesting job in UCD, so I asked my professor if he would be open to my taking a year out to go to L'Arche without my chances of getting the job being totally compromised. Though he said he would prefer me to be spending the year in Oxford or in Cambridge, he also said he would not hold it against me and he gave me his blessing. So in the early spring of 1982, I packed my bags and off I went to the green fields of France to this new style of Christian community based on the welcome of marginalised men and women with learning disabilities, called L'Arche, whose founder, Jean Vanier, had so deeply touched and inspired me.

I lived there in L'Arche Trosly (the founding community in France) for a period of two and a half years. After six months, I knew that I was not going to return to UCD and academic life. Something else was calling me to stay: my discovery of the gift of the marginalised person, and, in the specific context of my life in L'Arche, the gift of the person with a learning disability.

I remember sitting with a small young man called Eric who had a profound learning disability in the beautiful stone chapel in the village of Trosly one evening. Eric had been abandoned as a child at the age of two, and had spent most of his childhood and early adolescent years in a large psychiatric hospital before being welcomed to L'Arche. He was blind and was unable to walk or to speak when he first came to us. Yet he had a fighting spirit and a great desire to live life to the full, despite his past life of hurt and anguish. I had brought him to Mass and we had both just received communion together. Though he had been restless for most of the time during Mass, jumping up and down on my lap, he suddenly calmed down at communion time. He lay down on my lap and he began to sleep peacefully. I was touched by his total trust in me at that moment, the gift of his simplicity, his surrender. I knew with a deep inner certitude at that moment that I had found home, that I had found my people. Eric had made it clear to me, not by saying anything inspiring or persuasive or even by doing anything dramatic, but by simply lying down in my lap and falling asleep – the power of the powerless. I also knew then that the missing rib of emptiness that I had always carried within me was now being filled with a sense of belonging, and a curious sense of wholeness welling up from within me. It was as if I was discovering Yeats' 'unity of being' in what seemed to be a most unlikely source, in the gift and the paradox of the marginalised person.

I also met my wife, Maria, during those years in L'Arche Trosly in France. She had spent some time in Taizé, that inspiring interdenominational community founded by Brother Roger Schutz, and one of the brothers there had given her the address of L'Arche. Though Maria is a French citizen and was born in France, her mother is German and her father is Dutch. She quickly felt at home in the international atmosphere of L'Arche. She was drawn by the spiritual vibrancy of the community and was touched by the person with a learning disability. She was someone innately at home in community, more so than I. Slowly her journey and mine began to come together, and after a long period of discernment, we discovered that we were both called to a common vocation as a couple in L'Arche.

Both Eric and Maria, in their different ways, called me to discover the reality of choice, commitment and vocation. They called me to make the transition within my own life from someone who was seeking an inner path and a vocation to someone who was committed to a spiritual path and to living a vocation. They taught me something about the value and importance of commitment and of choosing a clear focus for my heart and of all the energy that would free up within me.

They taught me about what Jean Vanier calls covenant relationships, relationships which are based on both tenderness and faithfulness and which have a great inner power of healing because God is in some way present in them. I am grateful to them both for being my teachers and my guides in the ways of the heart.

I am grateful also to L'Arche for the gift of my marriage to Maria, and for the realisation that it is possible to be called as a couple to live a vocation in L'Arche, and, by extension, as lay people within the Church. Traditionally, one tended to think of vocation as a call made by God to an individual to the ordained or religious life (as a priest or a nun). It is exciting and, I think, significant that today God seems to be calling many lay people to a vocation within the Church, both as single people and as couples.

Today, some fifteen years after my initial 'year out' in L'Arche in France, I continue to walk the path of community life in L'Arche with Maria, our three children, and my brothers and sisters in community. I still believe as passionately as ever in the value and gift of people with a learning disability in our society, in our churches and in the mission that L'Arche has to support and enable them to discover and express their gift.

One particularly close friend of mine who often reminds me of this mission is a man called Danny Canty. Danny is a young man from the northside of Cork city who arrived on my doorstep one day with his dad, shortly after I had opened the first L'Arche house in Cork, twelve years ago. He and his dad had heard about the opening of L'Arche in Cork on the radio, and Danny wondered if there might not be a place with us for him, as he had already been through several services for people with mental handicaps without being able to keep his place in any of them. Danny was so open and upfront with me that day about his personal difficulties and his struggles that I could do nothing but warm to him and be touched by his story. Soon, Danny began to work with us one day a week in our garden project and about a year later he moved into the community and began to live with us.

Today, after twelve years of personal growth, of painful struggle and of building friendship and trust with me and many others in the community, Danny is living a more independent life in his own apartment. He is still a full member of the community, but he has chosen to live his sense of belonging in a more independent way. He is involved in a committed relationship with Maria, a young woman who also has a learning disability, who works in a nearby sheltered workshop and who lives at home with her parents. He continues to work full-time in our workshop.

Despite his strong and sometimes tough exterior, Danny is a man of the heart whose many gifts and qualities are shaped by his sensitivity and his strong sense of compassion. Because he has suffered so deeply in his own life (wounds linked with his feeling rejected because of his learning disability), he knows how to reach out to others in pain or distress. Though he would not describe himself as a 'religious' person, he is a deeply spiritual man, and sometimes he can be quite prophetic in what he says and does. I will leave the last word on my friend Danny to the priest and writer, Henri Nouwen, who spent the last ten years of his life ministering in the L'Arche community in Daybreak, Toronto, and who knew Danny from a summer holiday we spent together in L'Arche Trosly in France in 1985:

Tonight I spent a wonderful evening with the L'Arche group from Cork, Ireland, who are spending the month of August in Trosly. It is obviously easier for me to be among the Irish than among the French. The language helps, but also the easy camaraderie.

During evening prayer we sang simple songs, we listened to Danny, one of the handicapped men from Cork, who, with great difficulty, read from Jean Vanier's book, *I Meet Jesus*, and we prayed. Danny said, 'I love you, Jesus, I do not reject you even when I get nervous once in a while... even when I get confused. I love you with my arms, my legs, my head, my heart; I love you and I do not reject you, Jesus. I know that you love me, that you love me so much. I love you too, Jesus.' As he prayed I looked at his beautiful, gentle face and saw without any veil or cover his agony as well as his love. Who would not respond to a prayer like that?

I suddenly felt a deep desire to invite all my students from Harvard to sit with me there in that circle. I felt a deep love for all those men and women I had tried to speak to about Jesus and had often failed to reach. I wanted so much for all of them to sit and let Danny tell them about Jesus. I knew they would understand what I had not been able to explain.

A Journey to Daybreak*

Henri Nouwen

One afternoon, there was a ring at my doorbell, and a young woman stood at my door. She said, 'I am Jan Risse, and come to bring you greetings from Jean Vanier.' I had heard about Jean Vanier and the L'Arche community for mentally handicapped people, but I had never met him, spoken to him, written to him, or been in touch with his work. So I was quite surprised by these greetings and said, 'Well, thank you, but what can I do for you?' She said I could do nothing for her, that she had just come to bring me the greetings of Jean Vanier. I thought there must be some other reason for her visit, though, and tried to find out what it was, but she insisted that she came only to bring me greetings from Jean.

I found it hard to hear her. I kept thinking that her greetings were but the introduction to a request to give a lecture or a retreat or a sermon, or to write an article for a book. Convinced that bringing greetings wasn't all she came for, I tried once more. 'I appreciate hearing from Jean Vanier,' I said, 'but is there anything I can do for you?'

She smiled and said, 'Well, can I come in?' I realised then that I hadn't shown much hospitality and hastily invited her in, but explained that I had to leave shortly, as I had appointments. 'Just go ahead and keep your appointments,' she said, 'and I will spend some quiet time here until you return.'

When I returned that evening, I found my table set with a

---

* Sadly, Fr Nouwen died suddenly in 1996 after giving us permission to use this essay in this book but before its publication. He will be sadly missed by his family and by all his friends in the L'Arche community, both where he lived and worked in Daybreak, and worldwide.

beautiful linen cloth, nice plates and silverware, flowers, a burning candle, and a bottle of wine. I asked, 'What's all this?' Jan laughed and said she had decided to make me a nice meal. I asked her where she found all the things, but she gave me a funny look and said she'd found them right there, in my own kitchen, in my own cupboards. It was obvious that I didn't use them very often if I didn't even recognise them!

Then it dawned on me that something unique was happening. A stranger had walked into my home and, without asking me for anything, was showing me my own house.

Jan stayed for a few days, and did many more things for me. Then, when she left, she said, 'Just remember, Jean Vanier sends his greetings to you.'

A few years went by, and I forgot about Jan's visit. Then one morning, Jean Vanier phoned me. He said he was making a retreat in Chicago and wondered if I would like to join him. Again, for a moment, I thought he meant that he wanted me to give a talk there. But he insisted. He said, 'Henri, it is a silent retreat. We can just be together and pray.'

And that is how Jean and I met. In silence. We did speak a bit, but very little. In the years that followed, I made two visits to his community in France. During my second visit I made a thirty-day retreat and gradually came to the realisation that Jan Risse's visit had been the first of a series of events in which Jesus was responding to my prayer to be allowed to follow him more fully.

But the years between Jan's visit and my decision to become part of L'Arche were tumultuous and full of anxious searching. After ten years at Yale, I felt a deep desire to return to a more basic ministry. My trips to Latin America had set in motion the thought that I might be called to spend the rest of my life among the poor of Bolivia or Peru. So in 1983 I resigned from my teaching position at Yale and went to Bolivia to learn Spanish and to Peru to experience the life of a priest among the poor. My months there were so intense that I decided to keep a journal, which was later published under the title *Gracias!* I sincerely tried to discern whether living among the poor in Latin America was the direction to go. Slowly and painfully, I discovered that my spiritual ambitions were different from God's will for me. I had to face the fact that I wasn't capable of doing the work of a missionary in a Spanish-speaking country, that I needed more emotional support than my fellow-missionaries could offer, that the hard struggle for justice often left me discouraged and dispirited, and that the great variety of tasks and obligations took away my inner composure. It was hard to hear my friends say that I could do more for the South in the North than in the South and that my ability to speak and write was more useful among university students than among the poor. It became quite clear to me that idealism, good intentions and a desire to serve the poor do not make up a vocation. One needs to be called and sent. The poor of Latin America had not called me; the Christian community had not sent me. My experience in Bolivia and Peru had been very fruitful, but its fruits were not the ones I had expected.

About that time Harvard Divinity School invited me to join their faculty to teach Christian spirituality with a special emphasis on the spiritual aspects of liberation theology. I accepted with the conviction that I was called to a 'reverse mission', a mission from the South to the North, and that in this way I could realise my desire to serve the Church in Latin America. But I soon realised that the students had a greater need for spiritual formation than for information about the burning issues of the Latin American Church, and so my teaching quickly moved to more general areas of the spiritual life. Thus I found myself doing what I had done at Yale, only on a larger scale. Gradually I discovered that Harvard was not the place where I was called to follow Jesus in a more radical way; I was not really happy there, found myself somewhat sulky and complaining, and never felt fully accepted by the faculty or students. The signs were clear that I still had not found the way.

In the midst of all my doubts and uncertainties, the voices of

Jan Risse, Jean Vanier and L'Arche gained in strength. When I visited the L'Arche community in France I experienced a sense of at-homeness I had not experienced at Yale, in Latin America, or at Harvard. The non-competitive life with the mentally handicapped, their gifts of welcoming me regardless of name or prestige, and the persistent invitation to 'waste some time' with them opened in me a place that until then had remained unavailable to me, a place where I could hear the gentle invitation of Jesus to dwell with him. My sense of being called to L'Arche was based more on what I had to receive than on what I had to give. Jean Vanier said, 'Maybe we can offer you a home here.' That, more than anything else, was what my heart desired, even though I had never taken my desire seriously, and that gave me the first inkling that my prayer to follow Jesus more radically was being heard.

After I left Harvard and before I joined the L'Arche community of Daybreak in Canada, I spent a year mostly at Trosly-Breuil in France, where Jean Vanier first founded homes for people with mental handicaps, but I also made many excursions to Holland, Germany, Canada, the United States and other places. When I went to France, my hope was that L'Arche would prove to be the place where I would be called to follow Jesus. But I wasn't sure. In fact, the difference between the life of the university and the life at L'Arche proved to be so profound that I experienced many doubts about whether I would be able to make the jump.

During that year, I struggled with the question, 'How does one follow Jesus unreservedly?' In the past I had wanted to know where to go; now I knew where to go, but didn't really want to. Living and working with mentally handicapped people seemed precisely the opposite of what I had been trained and qualified to do. Everything else seemed more reasonable and useful than going to L'Arche. But still Jan Risse, Jean Vanier, my friends at L'Arche and, most of all, the handicapped people themselves kept saying, gently but persistently, 'Here is a home for you; maybe you need us.' All my desires to be useful, successful and productive revolted. Some of my trips away from L'Arche may have been an expression of that revolt. But whether I knew it at the time or not, they became part of the basic struggle to let go of old ways and to be led to 'where I rather would not go' (John 21:18). There was fear and confusion and loneliness in that first year of my journey to Daybreak, but I am convinced that that journey led me to the beginning of a new life.

When I finally made my decision and came to Daybreak I moved into a house with six handicapped people and their assistants and was warmly welcomed. One of the first things I was asked to do was to help Adam, a twenty-five-year-old man who does not speak, cannot let you know whether he likes his food or not, whether you are hurting him or not, whether he wants something or not. He seldom smiles. You are never sure if he recognises you. For all the basic things of life – dressing and undressing, walking, eating, going to the bathroom – he needs careful attention. Every day he suffers from epileptic seizures which often exhaust him so much that he needs hours of extra sleep to recuperate. In the beginning I was afraid to be with Adam. He is so fragile that I was always worried I would do something wrong. But gradually I came to know and love this stranger. As I gave him his bath, brushed his teeth, combed his hair, gave him his breakfast, and talked to him as if he could fully understand me, my fears were gradually cast out by emerging feelings of tenderness and care. I even began to miss him when I was away for a few days, and when home I came to enjoy just sitting with him, rubbing noses, caressing his face, or playing with his fingers. Thus a stranger became a friend.

Friendships also developed with the other handicapped members of the house. Bill started to give me hugs and John to take me out for a beer. Trevor began to give me flowers and Raymond to show me the new ways he had decorated his room. And even Rose, who is profoundly handicapped like Adam, volunteered some really beautiful smiles. It was not always easy to feel at home with these wounded people because there is so much pain and rejection hiding underneath the hugs, the beers, the flowers and the smiles, but what they give is so freely given that it creates deep, affective bonds.

But these bonds did not develop without great cost. It was the cost of facing my own handicaps. I had always known they were there, but I had always been able to keep them out of sight. But those who cannot hide their handicaps do not allow the assistants to hide theirs either. The director of the community and some of the long-term members, as well as the assistants in the house, offered me much support and guidance during my first months. They knew from their own experience that a life with handicapped people involves a radical self-confrontation, and they showed remarkable patience and care as I lived through my own fears and insecurities. Once I said to them, 'I first thought I came to help you care for handicapped people but now I feel as if you had accepted one more handicapped person among you.' Indeed, the facing of my own handicaps was the hardest battle of all.

First of all, I had to come to terms with the fact that I had not lived a family life since I was eighteen years old, and here I was faced with a large house to be cleaned, big meals to be cooked, countless dishes to be washed, and stacks of laundry to be done, not to mention shopping, doctors' appointments, book-keeping, transportation, and the never-ending need for repairs. After thirty-seven years of living in school where all these things were taken care of, family life made me aware of my lack of the most ordinary skills. Making a dinner for eleven people filled me with great fear and, except for sunny-side-up eggs, every request at breakfast, whether for pancakes, omelettes, French toast or waffles, threw me into utter confusion. Writing books and giving lectures seemed like easy hills to climb compared to the mountainous complexities of daily living. No wonder that I soon gave up on the idea that some of us are handicapped and others not. My handicaps were so blatantly visible in the face of what normal life is all about that I felt deeply grateful for every sign of sympathy, every smile of understanding, and, most of all, every helping hand. Maybe it was around these very down-to-earth kitchen type of things that I first started to experience the possibility of real friendship with handicapped people and their assistants. My own handicap became the way to it.

But this was obviously only the outer side of a much deeper struggle. As I entered more fully into the Daybreak community and tried to develop new and lasting relationships, I was faced with all the stresses of intimacy. My need for friendship and a deep sense of belonging had brought me to L'Arche. But the handicapped people who form the core of community are often most wounded in places of intimacy. They easily feel rejected, disliked, put aside or ignored and are very sensitive towards those who offer friendship, care, support and affection. The questions are always there: Is it real? Is it lasting? Can I trust it? It is no wonder that in such a context my own anguish concerning intimate relationships was brought into the open.

I vividly remember how one of the handicapped men did not want to say 'hello' to me after I had been absent for two weeks. While I felt a need to be welcomed back, he wasn't sure if I really was willing to become part of his life. And so our dark fears were rubbing up against each other and triggered off deep anguish in both of us. As he kept saying, 'I don't care that you are back, I don't need your gift. I have enough things already, don't bother me. I am busy...', my own deep fear of not being loved was brought to the surface, and to my own embarrassment I found myself crying uncontrollably, like a little child who feels rejected.

It was the affective wounds of the handicapped people in my own home that opened the door to my own wounded affectivity. Very soon, I was asking myself, 'Do I really care for these people? Am I really willing to make them the centre of my life? What do I really mean when I say to them, "I love you"? How faithful am I really? Am I capable of a lasting relationship? Or is my attention for these broken people little more than my way of feeling better about myself?' Very few stones remained unturned. Care, compassion, love for neighbour, promise, commitment and faithfulness. I turned and turned these concepts in my mind and heart, and sometimes it felt as though the spiritual house I had built up over the years was now proving to be made of cardboard and ready to go up in flames. The handicapped men and women and their assistants forced me to look at myself in ways that were very humbling. Often I doubted whether there was any struggle, and I felt quite poor in the face of it. It is hard to discover that I am very awkward in the ordinary tasks of life. But it is much more painful for me to be brought to the realisation that I am very weak and fragile precisely where I had thought I had the most to give.

But even this struggle proved not the most excruciating. Where I really was brought to my knees was at a place beyond questions about housekeeping skills, even beyond questions about true commitment. The most radical challenge came out of the question, 'Is Jesus truly enough for you, or do you keep looking for others to give you your sense of worth?' If anyone had asked me in the past, 'Who is the centre of your life?' I would have answered without much hesitation, 'Jesus, who called me to follow him.' But now I do not dare say that so easily. The struggle to become a full member of a community of faith has proved to be a struggle to let go of many idols along the way and to choose again and again to follow Jesus and him alone. Choosing life in community and choosing Jesus are increasingly appearing to me as two aspects of the same choice. And here my deepest handicap appeared.

When I came to Daybreak, I didn't come alone. Nathan, with whom I had developed a deep and nurturing friendship in Trosly, came with me. I came to Daybreak to become its pastor. He came to live as a part-time assistant while studying theology in Toronto. As I approached the new life in community, I came to think about my friendship with Nathan as the safe place in the midst of all the transitions and changes. I said to myself, 'Well, whatever happens, at least I have a friend to rely on, to go to for support, to be consoled by in hard moments.' Somehow I made Nathan the centre of my emotional stability and related to the life in community as something I would be able to cope with. In this way my dependence on Nathan prevented me from making the community the true centre of my life. Unconsciously, I said to myself, 'I already have a home. I do not really need another one.' As I entered community life more deeply, however, I became gradually aware that the call to follow Jesus unreservedly required me to look for God's guidance more in the common life with handicapped people than in a unique and nurturing friendship.

This discovery created such an excruciating inner pain that it brought me to the edge of despair. I had to change my ways of coming to a sense of being accepted so radically that it seemed as if I needed to have another personality to make this come true. When I had said 'yes' to the call of Daybreak to join the community as their priest, I hadn't realised how many painful 'nos' were included in that 'yes': 'no' to choosing the people you want to live with, 'no' to spending quality time with people you feel very close to, 'no' to a self-defined form of solitude, 'no' to centring my life in the beautiful and supportive friendship with Nathan. My many years of the independent and individualised life of a university professor had certainly not prepared me for this side of following Jesus. It led me to the second loneliness, a loneliness with Jesus in community. I discovered that this second loneliness was much, much harder to live than the loneliness resulting from physical or emotional isolation, because it is a loneliness not to be removed as a stumbling-block to full human maturity, but to be embraced as the way to follow Jesus to the end.

A young man I met on one of my trips told me about his own spiritual journey in a way that helped me to think about this second loneliness. He said, 'First, I was travelling on a highway with many other people. I felt lonely in my car, but at least I was not alone. Then Jesus told me to take an exit and follow a winding country road which was pleasant and beautiful. People who passed by greeted me, smiled and waved to me; I felt loved. But then, quite unexpectedly, Jesus asked me to take a dirt road, leave the car and walk with him. As we were walking we did not see anyone any more; although I knew that I was walking with Jesus, I felt very lonely and often in despair. I was tired and felt forgotten by my friends. Now it looked as if I was getting more lonely as I was getting closer to Jesus. And nobody seemed to understand.'

My life at Daybreak became increasingly an invitation to enter into this second loneliness. It is such a painful experience that I hesitate to write about it. It is a loneliness from which I know no friend can free me, even though I keep clinging desperately to such a friend. It is a loneliness that asks of me to throw myself completely into the arms of a God whose presence can no longer be felt and to risk every part of my being to what seems like nothingness. It is the loneliness of Jesus, who cries out, 'My God, my God, why have you forsaken me?'

In her novel *Henry and Cato*, Iris Murdoch writes of the great paradox that personal love, which seems beautiful and natural and good, has to be given up. 'After that,' she says, 'there's darkness and silence and space... the abyss of faith.' The last thing I ever expected from going to the Daybreak community was this truly abysmal experience of being ripped apart from the inside out. I expected to live with and care for mentally handicapped people, supported by a deep friendship and surrounded by a beautiful network of Christian love. I was not prepared to have to deal with a second loneliness.

But hesitantly and even reluctantly, I am coming to see the mystery that the community of Daybreak was given to me precisely to offer me a 'safe' context in which to enter into the second loneliness with Jesus. There is nothing charming or romantic about it. It is dark agony. It is following Jesus to a completely unknown place. It is being emptied out on the cross and having to wait for new life in naked faith.

But the same cross that calls for dying from what seems so

good and beautiful is also the place where a new spiritual community is being born. The death of Jesus was the dying of the grain destined to bear much fruit. My life will never be fruitful if I am not willing to go that same painful but hopeful route.

I express this with fear and trembling because I am just starting to see the light of a new day and I still do not know if I will have the courage to walk the long road ahead of me. But by writing this down I am able to look directly at my own words and that in itself is a step forward.

When, during my first year at Daybreak, I celebrated the thirtieth anniversary of my ordination, I didn't feel like having a party. Instead, I asked a few of the permanent members of the community to pray with me, to reflect with me on my vocation and to offer me some critical guidance. It was a very painful experience. I had to face all my handicaps directly, share them with my friends and reach out to God and the community for help. But it was also a very life-giving experience. Seeing my handicaps so clearly, those surrounding me offered all their support, guidance and love. This helped me to make them not just stumbling-blocks but gateways to solidarity with those who cannot hide their handicaps and who form the core of our community.

During this anniversary celebration, I made three promises for the years to come and asked the community to help me to be faithful to them. I want to conclude by writing down these promises, to articulate the way I see the road ahead of me.

First of all, I promised to pray more. If Jesus is the centre of my life, I have to give him much time and attention. In the past, my prayer has been introspective, but I want my life to be based on the reality of Jesus and not on the unreality of my own fantasies. It will be very hard to be faithful to this promise. There are countless pressures to do more important things than pray, but I know that only through long and persistent prayer will I be able to follow the one who asks me to walk the lonely road with him.

Second, I promised to do everything possible to come to know my own community better, to take meals in various community houses, to 'waste time' with my own people, talking, playing and praying with them. This is how I will come to know Jesus not only in the solitude of prayer but in the community of love. It will not be easy to be faithful to this promise either, since the temptation to search for consolation and comfort in the intimacy of a unique friendship is so great, especially during periods of distress and spiritual fatigue. But I now feel a strong invitation to let the community be my primary spiritual resource, and to trust that there I will find the spirit of God, the true consoler I have always been looking for.

Finally, I promised to keep writing. In the over-scheduled life of a community such as Daybreak it is hard to find the quiet hours necessary to write, but the call to come to Daybreak included the call to keep writing. It is through writing that my hidden life with God and the handicapped people can become a gift to the Church and the world.

I am glad to be at Daybreak, surrounded by people who want to keep me faithful to my promises. It is good to be here even though it is hard. I realise that I have just started on a long and arduous journey in which there will be not only many daybreaks, but also many nights. I know my faith will be tested. God's love is indeed, as Dorothy Day put it, a 'harsh and dreadful thing', but worth giving one's life for. As I travel with Jesus, he continues to remind me that God's heart is, indeed, infinitely greater than my own.

Journey towards Justice

Bernadette MacMahon DC

My story begins in a comfortable and happy home, in a south Dublin suburb. There were five of us children, and my parents were people of a strong, living faith. The atmosphere in the family was permeated by an awareness of the presence of a loving God who cared for people everywhere.

My mother was a gentle and compassionate woman. Her response, when people came knocking on our door seeking help, was consistently respectful and kind. When people asked for food, they were given part of the family meal. From her, we learned that poverty and hardship are not realities which people deserve or for which they should be blamed.

My father had an equally profound influence on my life. Because of his spirit of enquiry and love of literature we were exposed to poetry, myth and legend very early in life, and a world of wonder, beauty and promise became ours to imagine and experience. From my father we also learned to appreciate reality as it is but never to be satisfied with it. This encouragement to question and to visualise other ways of doing and being enabled me as I grew older to sense the gap between the vision of the world of which Jesus spoke and the world as experienced by many people.

My youngest brother has Down's syndrome. He came into the world as a much-loved baby brother, and it was some time before I realised that his development was slower than that of other babies. We knew him as a particularly engaging, loving and lovable little boy before we were aware that he had a handicap. My mother always held that our world was enriched by children like Tomás, who could draw out depths of love, generosity and goodness from people. She believed that God chooses the homes into which these children are born. The vulnerability and the courage, in face of illness and handicap, of this treasured little brother taught us not to categorise people according to disability. This was the beginning of my education about justice and the necessity to eliminate inequality and exclusion.

As I grew up, I studied St Luke's Gospel at school and came to a deeper and more personal knowledge of Jesus. When the time came to leave school, I had a growing conviction that only in God and in his vision for the world would I find all that I was seeking, and I felt myself drawn to spend my life in the service of God and of people in need. I fought against this idea, as I did not want to leave my family and my home, but in the end I applied to become a Daughter of Charity, half-hoping that I might fail the medical examination and so be let off the hook!

In fact I did pass the medical, and that is how I came to join my community, the Daughters of Charity. This community was founded in the seventeenth century by Louise de Marillac and Vincent de Paul, who brought together a group of women who were prepared to respond to the needs of people experiencing the terrible poverty brought about by war, famine and destruction. The example of their passionate and innovative response to human need continues to inspire and support me on my life's journey. They had a rare ability to see reality from the perspective of people who were marginalised by society and for them every poor person had the features of Christ.

I qualified as a teacher in England, and after a period spent teaching older children, I was sent to Sheffield, where I was expected to teach children between the ages of five and seven. At first I was dismayed, but I quickly came to realise that these children, many of whom came from poor homes, had only one chance of education, and that I was part of that chance.

My work as a teacher was mainly with children from materially deprived families who had difficulties in learning to read. They taught me, from the inside, about the reality of deprivation, and I discovered the Christ who identified himself with people who were rejected by the society of his day. It was from these young children that I gained an insight into the harsh reality of never having sufficient of the basic necessities of life and of being caught in a never-ending poverty trap.

Sean was one of my teachers. He did not go to birthday parties or on outings with his parents, so the typical reading book had no significance for him and, not surprisingly, he was not interested in learning to read from such books. But Sean was interested in 'scutting' – climbing on the backs of lorries and jumping off when the police were seen in the distance. So together we made a book about 'scutting'. Our second book was about a game called 'knock-off-and-pick-up'. Sean and his little brother would visit Woolworth's and while Sean knocked things off the counter and shelves with his elbow, his brother would crawl along the floor and pick up the fallen goods.

In time, Sean learned that he could read ordinary books too, and realised that he was good at football. He also acquired more productive ways of spending his time, but because of alcohol misuse at home, relations with his family deteriorated over the years, and Sean realised that he could not count on his parents to honour their promises. Watching that small boy cope with disadvantage, acquire skills, grow in self-esteem and then become disillusioned with the important adults in his life convinced me of the need for a considerable investment of finance and personnel in adult and community education if children are to be enabled to break out of the cycle of poverty. Sean's was not an isolated case. Helping other children from disadvantaged homes to read, befriending them and their families and seeing the many ways in which society oppresses people who are poor was a learning experience that had a lasting effect.

My work with children with learning and social problems led to postgraduate studies in educational psychology, so although at first I had been dismayed at the thought of teaching younger children, it led me eventually into an area that became a source of great interest and challenge to me. I had an opportunity to study alternatives to the system as well as the learning process. This period of study forced me to put many of my previously held ways of understanding and perceiving reality under the microscope and to question and examine them. All this had an impact on my religious beliefs and on my relationship with God, enabling me to reach a new level of critical awareness and maturity. I also became aware of a number of reductionist theories that can impoverish our understanding of what it is to be human, and I began to see that when the spiritual is ignored in policy-making, the social and community aspects of being human are often overlooked. It also became obvious to me that reductionist approaches to religion make Christianity boring and divorce it from the Gospel.

I returned to Ireland to help to care for my mother, who was by now widowed and in poor health. The three years I spent looking after my mother were among the most privileged of my life. It was intensely painful to watch my much-loved mother slowly deteriorating in health, but the sense of powerlessness that was part of those years helped me to identify with people who experience powerlessness in any of its many forms.

During this period I found work in Ireland at the Mater Dei Institute of Education, a third-level college for students studying religion, which at that point was in the early stages of development. As part of that highly qualified and dynamic staff, I had a valuable opportunity to take part in a search for a more contemporary way of communicating the Gospel to young people. It became apparent to me, as I visited the schools to supervise students who were doing their teaching practice, that teaching religion in some of the marginalised areas of Dublin constituted a particular challenge. How does one speak of a loving God to young people who, because of their life experience, may have literacy problems or short concentration spans, or who may be alienated from all authority figures? In the course of my work I interviewed young people from privileged backgrounds as well as those from homes that were materially disadvantaged, and the contrast in the social, educational and economic realities experienced by these youngsters brought me once more up against systems that have their own momentum and dynamic, and in which people who are poor are always the losers. Education, which is often regarded as an important means of eliminating disadvantage, often consolidates disadvantage because of competitive structures.

At one period of my life I was appointed to a community in a large centre that catered for people with a mental handicap, and although I did not work directly with the residents, I came to make friends with a number of them. One of these friends, Susan, sometimes has difficulty in making herself understood, although she is a good communicator. One day I asked her a question, but I could not comprehend her answer. I knew that Susan did not like to have to repeat herself, so I tried to guess the word. After five or six unsuccessful attempts, Susan said with some frustration, 'My God, you are stupid!' I tried a few more times, and then had to give up. 'I'm sorry, Susan,' I said. Susan put her arm around me and said, 'Never mind, you can't help it.' From Susan's point of view, the limitations of so-called normal people created difficulties for her and people like her, but she was willing to forgive us.

Over the years, and through my relationships with people like Susan and my little brother, I learned that the principal difference between the person with a mental handicap and the so-called normal person is that the handicap of the latter is less obvious. In the presence of people with a handicap, one becomes conscious of a wonderful capacity for love, a generosity of spirit and sheer enjoyment of life. At the same time one also becomes aware of the pain caused by lack of respect or recognition, what Jean Vanier calls the pain in the heart of every person with a mental handicap, the pain of knowing you are different and possibly a disappointment to your family. There is also the constant uncertainty of realising that you are completely dependent on others for literally everything of importance in your life.

In addition to my work with students and young people, I also gained experience, through my work with my order, of life in Africa, and I was constantly inspired by the love and utter selflessness that characterised the work of the sisters there. One story that I think illustrates this is about a young man who met a sister (from another congregation) on a train. He asked her if she knew a particular sister of our congregation, who was a founding member of an innovative project for young people who had dropped out of school and society. 'She is the only person who ever loved me,' was how he described her.

The compassion, determination and creativity of sisters here in Ireland and in Africa is a constant source of inspiration and encouragement to me. It is not possible to draw comparisons between poverty in a western country and poverty in developing countries, but the differences between relative and absolute poverty became painfully obvious to me in Africa. In one country I visited, one in three children dies before the age of five. In some African countries there are pockets of dire poverty, but here the whole country was in a state of total destitution, although multinational companies continue to make large financial gains from their mineral resources. On one occasion when I visited, a hospital run by our sisters had to close and the people had to flee, because of civil disquiet and rebel activity. I will never forget those evacuation journeys, some of them at night, watching the people carrying all their belongings on their heads and their children on their backs, walking in almost complete silence. I was horrified to hear, after I had returned to Ireland, that our European co-workers – an Irish parish priest and a Dutch doctor with his wife and three-year-old daughter – had been ambushed and murdered. Miraculously, four of our sisters who had been part of the same convoy had escaped being killed. In the wake of this tragedy, which was a dark hour for our community, the people of that country asked that we in Ireland should take action regarding the sale of arms to Africa, pointing out that it was European or American guns that had killed our workers. The suffering which this tragedy brought the different families, ourselves, and the people who are still refugees from their village gave us a profoundly painful awareness of the anguish that is experienced daily by people in developing countries.

I will always remember my first visit to a prison in another African country where Irish Daughters of Charity work with prisoners, bringing them care and friendship. The sight of the inhuman conditions in which the prisoners were living left me numb with shock and horror. Many people in these prisons spent years of their lives waiting for trial and it is always those without financial resources or influence who have to wait longest. One of the sisters who took a stand against the injustices of prison life was not allowed to continue her work. While meeting the prisoners, in particular those who were awaiting execution, always left me with strong feelings of anger and helplessness, the spirit, dignity and courtesy that people showed in such appalling circumstances extended my understanding of human greatness.

I found the same courage and steadfastness among the people, and particularly among the women, when I visited our communities in west Belfast, where there was considerable poverty and unemployment, in the 1970s and 1980s. Meeting people in their homes after they had been raided by the army and visiting people in prison made me view the problems of Northern Ireland always in terms of the suffering of families, who were not only poor but who also experienced anger, frustration and powerlessness. In Northern Ireland, injustice and exclusion take on very obvious forms.

In my travels to Britain and the United States in recent years, I have become aware of a hardening of attitudes towards people who have to rely on welfare. It seems that there has been less focus on the redistribution of wealth and more on the desire on the part of the rich to become very rich. Here in Ireland too – although as a nation we tend to be caring – there is an urgent need for change in some of our social and economic systems. A number of these systems produce wealth and poverty at the same time and the structures that underpin our statutory services in many cases consolidate rather than reduce the gap between the rich and the poor.

All my experiences in Ireland, in Africa and in England led me to conclude that, although it is important to respond to immediate human needs, it is equally important to take action to change the structures that cause poverty and disadvantage. Experience also shows that people who are working face-to-face with men, women and children who are poor or marginalised, though they are promoting a more just society by their work, are frequently too busy to engage in a sustained and systematic way with the causes of the problems that they encounter. The structures that exclude people, that make them feel powerless and oppressed, that prevent them from participating in a meaningful way in society and that as a consequence alienate people, are not inevitable outcomes of living in today's world. These things can be changed, but too frequently they are simply accepted. It is disturbing to discover that one can help to create or maintain economic and social structures that make it impossible for people in Ireland and elsewhere to live with dignity.

In 1995 the joint commission of the St Vincent de Paul Society, the Vincentian Congregation and the Daughters of Charity established the Vincentian Partnership for Justice as an initiative for economic and social change, tackling poverty and exclusion. The vision of the Partnership is as follows:

> Recognising the dignity of the human person, made in the image of God, and Jesus' particular identification with people who are excluded by society, our vision is a more just society in which the rights, responsibilities and development of all people are promoted. The Vincentian Partnership for Justice seeks to transform the structures that give rise to inequality, poverty and exclusion.

The rhythm of my life to date has been one of encounter with people for whom the powerlessness, frustration and alienation caused by poverty and exclusion are part of daily life, a deepening awareness of the urgent need for structural change if the gap between rich and poor is not to widen and cause further suffering as well as unrest, and a growing conviction that 'action on behalf of justice and participation in the transformation of the world are a constituent element' of being a Christian (1971 Synod on Justice in the World). It seemed natural then that, when I was given the opportunity, I should offer to work with the Vincentian Partnership for Justice. I am privileged to be allowed to work with this group and am pleased to be part of an effort to create an alternative future for the third of the Irish people who live below the poverty line and for people in developing countries where human rights and dignity are often grossly violated. Dorothy Day warned against being 'tourists in the world of people who are poor', but because of their friendship and solidarity, many members of the Vincentian Partnership are received as 'naturalised citizens' in the world of people who are excluded from meaningful participation in Irish society. It is this proximity to people who are poor which we hope will give a specific character to the work of the Vincentian Partnership for Justice.

My life's journey – outward and inward – began in a home in which a little brother with Down's syndrome was particularly cherished, and in which I saw respect, compassion and practical help for all people. In the course of my life as a Daughter of Charity, I have discovered the compassionate Christ who chose specifically to identify himself with people who were oppressed by poverty, sickness or exclusion, and learned about the passionate response to human need that was the inspiration for the founders of my community. In my work with children from materially deprived families I have learned about the harsh reality of living in poverty and being trapped for life in exclusion and disadvantage, and, in Ireland and Africa, I have been exposed to many forms of poverty, marginalisation, destitution and the consequences of grave injustice. I have discovered that in opening my heart to men, women and children who are excluded by society because of poverty, handicap or powerlessness, I have been changed and am changing. I do not know the way ahead, and I have no idea where it will end, but I believe that the God who has led me this far will continue to be with me, and like Patrick Kavanagh I 'claim my inheritance', which comes from the past, is for now and the future, and which includes many gifts:

- The gift of being touched by the compassion of my mother and love of enquiry and literature of my father
- The gift of love and friendship of my brothers and sisters and the special gift of my brother with Down's syndrome
- The gift of a call to follow Christ in the community of the Daughters of Charity, and within its charism of finding Christ in his brothers and sisters who suffer because of poverty and injustice
- The gift of sisters in whose lives I so often glimpse the presence of Christ living, loving and working among and with people marginalised by society
- The gift of being taught by children and others of the harsh reality of poverty
- The gift of many opportunities to know people in Ireland, Africa and elsewhere who, in spite of great suffering, manifest the nobility and richness of the human spirit
- The gift of the companionship and collaboration of many people who have inspired, challenged and enriched me in countless ways
- The gift of being drawn to be part of an effort to create a more just world

And above all

- The gift of God's love and of life, which is always full of mystery and of signs of his presence

CONVERSION TO COMPASSION

Max Oliva SJ

My mother taught me the value of being compassionate. She did this by example. Although she was from a wealthy family, she had a genuine concern for those who were economically less fortunate than she. When I was a child, she often took me with her as she brought food or clothing to those in need. Later, as I entered my late teens and then went through college, I lost this sense for the 'underdog', but I was to recover it when I joined the Jesuit Order.

As a Jesuit, I have been privileged to spend time in a variety of countries and cultures. In every situation I have learned from the people. They have taught me to appreciate their customs and values, they have deepened my compassion by sharing with me their stories of being oppressed, and they have helped me to become a better human being. Over the years, I have come to view my encounters – with African American people, among destitute people in Calcutta, India, with those who are economically poor in Tijuana, Mexico, and with Travellers in Dublin – as 'conversion to compassion' experiences. This is so because in most of these situations I have had to face prejudices within myself from which I needed to be freed in order truly to love the people and thus feel compassion for them in their circumstances. I have discovered that prejudice is a block to one's heart. To be freed from such an obstacle demands conversion.

While I was studying for the priesthood, I felt drawn to the plight of Black people in the United States. This was in the late 1960s, during the Civil Rights Movement. Since I grew up in a white community, I decided to begin my inquiry in a Black inner city neighbourhood near where I was living at the time. I went from house to house with a simple question, 'What is it like to be Black and live in this city?' At first I was turned away before I could utter the question, but finally a Black woman in her late twenties answered the door and invited me in. When she heard the purpose of my visit, she had me sit down and proceeded to tell me her life story! It was a graced time as my mind and my heart slowly opened to understanding and compassion not only for her but also for a people.

I supplemented these visits by taking a course in Black history and by reading a variety of books on the African American experience. Finally, I moved into a parish in a Black neighbourhood. There my education and appreciation of the people accelerated rapidly, as I met people in their homes and on the street. I developed a job programme for Black men, drawing on the experience I had before I joined the Jesuits when I worked in the business world. I came to the decision to undertake this ministry after considering the needs of the community, especially in the areas of education, employment, health care, and relations with the police. Realising that I could not meet all these needs, I chose the one that most closely fit my own talents. I decided to concentrate my efforts on behalf of the men because at that time they were more discriminated against than Black women in the job market.

As I became more and more involved in the employment scene, both by meeting unemployed men and employers who might hire them, my basic interest shifted from that of charity, that is, giving food and other goods to those in need, to social justice: trying to change the social structures that kept the people in poverty. I realise that both charity and justice are needed, for people need the basic goods of life to have the energy to seek work. My attention, however, slowly drifted more to justice. In the process, some prejudices against Black people emerged in me. I am of Italian-Irish ancestry and I was dismayed to find that most racist whites I encountered in the business world were of either Italian or Irish ancestry. This was especially true in the unions. I was forced to face my own myths and stereotypes about Black people. At times, I was like the blind man who went to Jesus to be healed, except my blindness was the irrational sin of prejudice. Over time, the prejudices dropped by the wayside and the more this happened the more effective my work became.

Two curious and unexpected insights came to me in the first year of my living and working in the Black community. Both had a connection to my father. My father suffered from a low self-image at times and he sometimes took this out on his children by putting us down, without really meaning it, in order to build himself up.

As a consequence of this, I grew up with an inferiority complex, which enabled me, in a small way, to have a special sensitivity to the Black men I met, who experienced being put down by the white community in a myriad ways. 'At a time when most of us don't trust white folks', a Black man from the neighbourhood said to me, 'We get along with you fine.' It seems that my feelings of being inferior had connected, in solidarity, with his and others'. God works in strange ways: it was my weakness that became my greatest strength.

The second insight is connected to the first. Due to my experience of being oppressed at times by my father I was able to feel, at a profound level, the oppression of Black people at large. Although the cause of my feelings was different from theirs, the result to my psyche was similar. It became what I call a 'moment of solidarity'. I felt this especially when I listened to Gospel music. I cried through most of the movie, *The Colour Purple*, the poignant story of a Black woman's experience of oppression and resurrection.

I had the opportunity to go to South Africa twice, both

times before the end of apartheid. The feelings of compassion and solidarity that had been formed in me through my contact with African American people had a resonance in my heart with the African people in South Africa. In fact, I was living in an African American parish the first time I went to South Africa. The day before I left was a Sunday. At the main Mass, the pastor invited me to kneel before the people who then extended their hands and gave me a blessing to send me safely on my way. It was quite a moment.

The insights I gained while working in the African American community over a period of fifteen years, sometimes full-time and the rest part-time, were to find a fruitful outlet in a summer programme for Jesuit brothers and priests that I directed. The programme was called Compassion for Justice. It was a seven-week insertion experience among people who are economically poor. The main components were direct experience in inner city parishes, soup kitchens, and convalescent homes; social analysis, or reflection on the causes of people's poverty; and faith reflection, linking the Bible to the participants' experience. The programme was designed in such a way as to respond to the 1971 Synod, 'Justice in the World', which stated, among other things:

> Action on behalf of justice and transformation of the world fully appear to us as a *constitutive* (emphasis added) dimension of the preaching of the Gospel or, in other words, of the Church's mission for the redemption of the human race and its liberation from every oppressive situation.

Part of my job as Director of Companions for Justice was to visit each man, at the site, accompany him for a day, and then help him to integrate what he was experiencing. As a result of these visits, I came to the conclusion that there are many ways in which even good-hearted people resist the poverty they are witnessing and the challenges inherent in it. I came up with the following 'blocking mechanisms' that one might encounter within oneself:

— *spiritualism*: when we interpret the poverty we are seeing solely from a detached spiritual perspective and, thus, find it very difficult to conduct a structural analysis of the impoverishment in order to understand the causes of the poverty.

— *intellectualism:* when we understand the situation of the people intellectually, but are unable or unwilling to engage our hearts in the work or in a reflection on the work.

— *personalism:* when we give ourselves completely to the persons with whom we work, usually on a one-to-one basis, but are not interested in a reflective and intellectual analysis of the situation.

— *comparison:* when we compare the poverty we are seeing with more dismal conditions in other cities or countries we have been to or have read about. The result is a tendency to miss the depth of oppression that is right in front of us, forgetting that poverty is relative, that is, if the effects of injustice are present, they are just as dehumanising to people where we live as elsewhere, although not perhaps to the same degree.

— *blaming the victim:* when we blame the person caught in the cycle of poverty for the state he or she is in, regarding that person as simply inferior, generally defective, morally unfit, lazy or shiftless; if a person is unemployed we say it's because he or she really doesn't want to work, and so forth. We give no attention to unjust social structures that are in need of reform and of systemic change.

– *our personal history:* when a situation reminds us of something painful from our past, for example, a relative who is an alcoholic, and this causes us to avoid, reject, or misjudge the people we see who are down and out as the result of drinking too much liquor.

These 'blocking mechanisms' can stifle or, at the very least, diminish the possibility of conversion of the heart to compassion and commitment, unless they are detected and faced. I have found it important to talk out my emotional and intellectual reactions to oppressive situations with someone who is knowledgeable in this area, to help me get past whatever resistance I am experiencing.

A summer in Calcutta

The English theologian and scripture scholar, William Barclay, describes the first Beatitude, 'Blessed are the poor in spirit; the reign of God is theirs,' as the poverty which is 'beaten to its knees'. I was to witness this depth of destitution during the summer of 1977. I went to live and work in Calcutta, India, for two-and-a-half-months. There I lived with the Brothers of the Missionaries of Charity, founded by Mother Teresa. The brothers work among the poorest of the poor, those who live and die on the pavements and in the train stations of Calcutta, lepers and people with mental or physical handicaps.

During my summer in Calcutta, I faithfully wrote out my reflections in a journal. Because of the intensity of the experience, I sometimes found myself writing three times a day. I had heard a lot about this city of thirteen million people (at that time). I had heard that over 250,000 people were forced to live on the streets because of a shortage of housing. I had heard how emotionally overwhelming the sight of so many destitute people was. I had heard how some westerners were only able to stay a few days before the sight of such misery drove them out. And so I left my home in California with the gnawing fear that I would not be able to survive the summer there. I am the sort of person who needs people to help me make sense of what I am experiencing, and my primary anxiety was that I would not have anyone to process these experiences with and that I would either go crazy or return home earlier than planned.

I left San Francisco in early June. I chose to stop in Hong Kong for a five-day stay, as a way of 'getting my feet wet' in a part of the world I had never been to before – Asia. The day before I left California, these words from the Mass gave me encouragement and hope: 'We have a spirit who makes us strong, loving and wise'. I prayed, especially, for an increase in the first of these gifts. In Hong Kong, I had my first opportunity to experience some of the constants of Asia: teeming masses of people and the consequent lack of privacy, the industriousness of men, women and, sometimes, children, working in tiny shops manufacturing everything imaginable, and the energy-sapping heat which kept me wringing wet all day. It was while I was in this hard-working city that I came across this prayer by the Korean, Kim Kwan Suk, which was to be of great encouragement to me during the entire summer:

> Give me hope
> to look forward
> to happy tomorrows.
> Give me courage
> to face the hardships
> without losing hope.

Give me faith
so that the joy of receiving Christ
will lead me to serve my fellow human beings.
Give me appreciation
for the gifts I have received
that I might use them responsibly
daring to give
friendship, service and love.

I arrived in Calcutta at midnight and was met at the airport by three of the brothers of the Missionaries of Charity. As we drove through the streets on our way to their novitiate, which would be my home for the summer, I could see many families sleeping on sidewalks. My exposure to a new kind of poverty had begun.

In his book, *Calcutta*, Geoffrey Moorhouse has these rather sober reflections on the city:

> It is the easiest thing in the world to come close to despair in Calcutta. Every statistic that you tear out of the place reeks of doom. Every half-mile can produce something that is guaranteed to turn a newcomer's stomach with fear or disgust or a sense of hopelessness. Yet for anyone with the wilful staying power to remain through that first awful week when Calcutta is driving him or her away with shock, with nausea, with resentment and with plain gut-rotting funk, a splendid truth about this city slowly dawns upon their perceptions and understanding. It is that although they will surely never before have encountered so much that is deadly in any one place, they have never been confronted with so much life either. It pulsates and churns around one wherever one goes, it swirls in every direction. Though it marches angrily and viciously, it also laughs idiotically and infectiously. While

it is staggering miserably, it is also wondering thoughtfully. It is reproducing itself minute by minute, it is thriving and proudly brandishing itself. It dominates.

The first four days in Calcutta were critical ones for me. Upon them, the entire summer depended. On the first afternoon, I sat on the third-floor balcony of the novitiate and looked out at the city. I observed streets filled with people; I saw beggars waiting at our front door – men, women, and children, poorly clothed, hoping for food; in the distance I could see mechanical cranes used for loading and unloading the ships on the River Hooghly; I noticed how bleak the buildings looked, weather-beaten from the monsoons and the heat. As I sat there, I began to feel sad, confused and discouraged. I decided to go to a talk being given to the novices by the then general superior of the brothers, Brother Andrew. What occurred at this conference was an experience of God's presence that was to be repeated many times, in various guises, throughout the summer.

Andrew's talk was on the discernment of spirits. As he spoke, I began to understand the causes of my unrest. I had been told that the following day I would be going with some of the novices to Mother Teresa's home for dying destitutes. I was concerned about what possible effect this place of intense suffering would have on me. Other causes came to mind as well: the widespread poverty I was beginning to experience, the newness of country, culture, language, life-style of the brothers (sleeping on a bedroll on the floor, not having any privacy, eating very simple food, no air conditioning – not even a fan – no shower, hot water or toilet paper, few chairs in the house, no radio or television, and no rugs on cement floors). Earlier in the day I had been inclined to put my confidence in memories of people and places back home as a way out of the emotional discomfort I was experiencing.

Listening to Andrew, I began to substitute thoughts on the power of God, and gradually the sadness, confusion and discouragement vanished.

On the morning of the second day, I went with three of the brothers and two other guests to the home for dying destitutes, otherwise known as 'Nirmal Hriday', which means 'Pure Heart'. There is simply no way to describe what met my eyes when I walked into this place. It was like what the liberating soldiers must have seen when they walked into Dachau at the end of World War II. Emaciated and malnourished men, women and children were lying on cots, women with tuberculosis, others with ugly cuts and sores, some dying before my eyes, others in various stages of recovery. It was a heart-breaking sight. The boys and men were in one section of the building, the girls and women in another. Soon after we arrived, a Jesuit from Austria, also volunteering for the summer, handed me a pan of warm water, a bar of soap and a towel, and showed me how to wash the boys and men on their cots. We washed all who were too weak to tend to themselves. Many of these people had been found dying on the streets of Calcutta and were brought to Nirmal Hriday to die with dignity. After the washing I helped to distribute food to the boys and men, giving each person two pieces of bread, a peeled banana, and a cup of milk. Mother Teresa's sisters were doing the same in the women's section. By this time it was mid-morning and there was a break in the work. I wandered over to a quiet area and began reading a prayer that was posted on a pillar. As I read I could see the various people I had recently washed and fed. Here is the prayer I read:

> Dear Lord, the Great Healer
> I kneel before you,
> since every good and perfect gift
> must come from You.

I pray, give skill to my hand, clear
vision to my mind, kindness and
sympathy to my heart.
Give me singleness of purpose,
strength to lift at least a part of
the burden of my suffering fellowmen and women
and a true realisation of the
privilege that is mine.
Take from my heart all guile and
worldliness that with the simple faith of a
child I may rely on you.

At this moment of quiet reflection, the enormity of what I had seen and done that morning hit me. Tears rolled down my cheeks. I found myself unable to resume the work schedule. I asked a Jesuit from Malta, who was also staying with the brothers, to show me how to get back to the novitiate, as we had come by bus. He knew exactly how to respond because he had been through the same reaction when he first arrived. Back at the house I tried to cope with the emotions stirred up in me by the morning's events. Brother Andrew was there. I joined him for a cup of tea and broke down and cried until there were no tears left. He listened in silence, ministering powerfully to me just by his presence. He finally suggested I take the afternoon and the next day off and get to know the city. He told me of other places I could go to volunteer if I decided not to return to Nirmal Hriday. He left the decision in my hands.

I took Brother Andrew's advice and spent the afternoon walking in the neighbourhood. On my way home I spied a Catholic church. I went in and immediately felt consoled. I went to bed early that night, emotionally and physically spent from the experiences of the day, a day in which I had seen 'poverty beaten to its knees'.

The third day began with Mass. I prayed for courage and strength. Some thoughts came to me about returning to California, but the main tenor of my thinking was: 'I want to stay here no matter what happens. God has invited me to Calcutta for the summer, he will see me through.' The celebrant, in one of his Offertory petitions, prayed that when we feel our weakness we might not become discouraged, but realise that God can do magnificent things through it. I took hope from these words. Later, as I sat on the balcony, I heard a girl's voice calling me. I looked across the street and there, standing in a small patio, was a teenage girl. She asked me to come over and join her and her family for tea. It was just what I needed, to be in a normal family situation with Indian people. I gladly accepted. The family lived in one room, yet, despite the frugality of their living conditions, there was a dignity and a hospitality about them that deeply impressed me. I was to get to know them quite well during the rest of the summer. They ministered to me often by their friendship.

Day four fell on Sunday, the feast of Corpus Christi. That morning at prayer, I was led to read a passage from St Paul's Second Letter to the Corinthians (4:1, 16-18):

> Because we possess this ministry through God's mercy, we do not give in to discouragement… We do not lose heart, because our inner being is renewed each day even though our body is being destroyed at the same time. The present burden of our trial is light enough, and earns for us an eternal weight of glory beyond all comparison. We do not fix our gaze on what is seen but on what is unseen. What is seen is transitory; what is unseen lasts forever.

Brother Andrew, who is also a priest, was the main celebrant at Mass that day. In his homily, which was centred on the multiplication of the loaves and fishes (Luke 9:11-17), he spoke of the surplus of food left after everyone present had eaten. He pointed out that if we had been in Jesus' situation we would have made sure that all the baskets were clean and there were no leftovers. Not so Jesus. Not only did everyone have enough bread and fish to eat, but they had more than they needed. Andrew said, 'For me this means that God provides not only what we need but more than we need.' This reflection really hit home with me. I realised at that moment that I had to believe and trust that God would give me what I needed to survive and thrive in Calcutta. It was a moment of utter helplessness and absolute confidence in God's providential love. One of my primary concerns before leaving home was who I would talk to in order to process what I would see and experience. Looking back on that summer, one of the key memories has to do with the number of people I encountered, in various and unexpected places, who generously met my need to be listened to. The journal I kept at that time is filled with exclamations of 'God provides more than I need!!!' The grace from this experience has deepened over the years and the memory of what happened to me in Calcutta has sustained and strengthened me in many situations since. God provides not only what we need but more than we need – to do what we are called to do.

The following morning I returned to the home for dying destitutes where I worked frequently for the rest of my stay in Calcutta.

Facing my prejudices
I have been working as a part-time pastor of a small mission church in Tijuana, Mexico, since 1987. I say part-time, because my primary ministry for the past sixteen years has been in giving retreats, which I do in California and elsewhere in the United States as well as in other English-speaking countries. Some have phrased what I do as 'time-tithing', that

is, setting apart quality time to be with people who are economically poor or marginalised in some way. For me, this is a technical term for doing something I love: being with people who are materially poor.

I have come to truly love Mexican people. It has been a journey from emotional blindness to new light. Here is the story.

In the summer of 1982, I lived and worked in Tijuana for seven weeks. I stayed at Casa de los Pobres (House of the Poor), a multi-service facility, directed by Mexican Francisan sisters, that offers food, clothing and medical care to the very poor in Tijuana. The population of the city is a million and a half, at least half of whom struggle to make a living. Tijuana's city limits border the United States, a modern rich man and Lazarus experience, and is only a half-hour drive from where I live in San Diego, California.

Prior to 1987 I had had some contact with people of Mexican descent in California, but I had never lived in a Hispanic neighbourhood. About ten days into the summer experience, I discovered, much to my humiliation, that I had three distinct prejudices against Mexicans. After all those years working in the African American community, I thought I was free of prejudice. Not so. Here was another ethnic group, different from my own, that I needed to learn how to love.

One prejudice came from a memory of something that had happened to me when I was twelve years old, an incident that concerned a Mexican. Somehow this event had unconsciously soured my outlook on all Mexican people. As I sat and reflected on the possible causes of my emotional blindness, I asked the Lord for a healing of the memory in my unconscious.

First I had to let the painful memory surface. This is the difficult part of the healing process because some memories are too painful to remember. When I did this prayer I was amazed to find a lifting of this burden to my heart almost immediately. I could feel the difference, a kind of lightness of my spirit.

Upon further reflection and self-questioning, two additional prejudices came to mind, two stereotypes about Mexican people: that they are dirty and lazy. Facing and being freed of these involved a more lengthy process. I realised that the source of the 'they are lazy' stereotype came from films and photographs I had seen which often portrayed Mexican men sitting down or leaning against a wall with their sombreros tipped to cover their eyes, resting, as if this is what they do all the time, instead of just after the midday meal. With regard to the second misconception, 'they are dirty', I had somehow got it into my head, as a child, that white people were clean because they were white, and brown people were not because of the colour of their skin. I decided to look deliberately for the opposite of these two stereotypes, rightly judging – as it turned out – that if I could change my thoughts, my feelings would follow.

There were so many daily examples of the industriousness and cleanliness of the people, I had never very far to look. I saw men and women pushing carts, selling tamales, cooked corn, ice cream, and other food items. I witnessed Mexican Indian women selling trinkets they had made at home to the tourists in the downtown area. One day, as I was emerging from a visit to St Francis' Church in the centre of the city I saw six men sitting on the kerb across the street from the church. Each was holding a kind of large hammer. Occasionally when a car passed by, one of the men would run out into the street and shout something to the driver. Since at that time I did not speak much Spanish, I did not know what the men were yelling. That evening, back at Casa de los Pobres, I asked one of the sisters about this strange event I had seen. She laughed and said, 'Oh, Padre, those men fix dents in cars! When they see a car with a dent in it, they run out to ask if the driver would like to have it mended right there, at a much lower price than he or she would pay in an auto repair shop.' After that experience, 'they are lazy', disappeared from my consciousness.

As I came to know the people, both at the centre and in their homes, I discovered that the only dirty people were those who were so poor they could not afford to purchase water. In the mornings I often saw the women sweeping the area in front of their little houses. I watched at Mass how even the poorest of the poor came in their best outfits. Gradually, this prejudice slipped away too.

As the summer progressed, my heart opened more and more. Of course, I was also seeing other qualities of the people: their spontaneous affection, warm hospitality, their extended families, care for the elderly and infirm and so on. One day it simply occurred to me that I had fallen in love with the people. God had led me from the darkness of my prejudice to the light of friendship with the people.

One important lesson I learned from the summer in Tijuana is that prejudice is a block to one's heart. If I am prejudiced against some person or group I will not be able to feel compassion with them in their struggles nor have the heart to love them. A second important insight has to do with compassion. As Henri Nouwen points out, compassion means being at one with the other, able to see life through the other's eyes. An important consequence of the healing that happened in me is that I have a far deeper understanding and empathy for those who enter the United States illegally from Mexico. They do so in order to escape grinding poverty and to seek new opportunities for their families. I know at first hand the dreadful effects of their high unemployment and under-employment, the low high school graduation rate of their children, who must go out and make a living to help the family to survive, the diseases they suffer, like tuberculosis, meningitis and leprosy, many of which have been eradicated in the United States. I have seen the white blemishes on children's faces that indicate worms in their intestinal tract from bad water. I have watched mothers pick the lice from their children's scalp. In other words, I now see the Mexican-United States Border from both sides.

My vulnerability in Tijuana is that I do not speak Spanish fluently. I am able to celebrate Mass and hear confessions in Spanish, but sometimes I get lost for a word, or a phrase, in my homilies. This used to be embarrassing. Now I see it as a gift, as I must depend on the parishioners for help, in spite of all my education and academic achievements. We often have 'shared homilies' as they help me out of my weakness. These are moments of solidarity with the people, who often feel powerless in other ways.

Compassion, like any other human dynamic, can grow or wither. There is a form of contemplation-to-compassion that I sometimes practise in the Colonia district, where the mission church I now work at is situated. I sit on the side of a hill and gaze at the unpaved, rough roads. I contemplate the simple dwellings of the people, the lack of trees and flowers, except for Señor Romero's pretty garden, the outdoor toilet facilities. Old abandoned cars rust away here and there, some of the houses are jumbled together, clothes are hanging out to dry on makeshift fences, and in the midst of it all children are playing. During this time of reflection, I try not to analyse what I am seeing, for I have been in most of the houses I see. I simply want to *be* there, drinking in the scene, letting God speak to my heart through the reality of the poverty, allowing my mind and my heart to open more fully to the life of the people.

As I mentioned at the beginning, my retreat work has taken me to a variety of countries and cultures. On these journeys, God continually places me in close proximity to people who are marginalised in some way. I have learned over the last thirty years to approach each new culture with reverence.

Each, I believe, is a manifestation of the wonderful creativity of our God. For example, in 1982 I began giving retreats in Ireland. Soon after I arrived I was introduced to the Traveller community in Finglas, Dublin. At St Joseph's Training Centre I met a group of teenage girls who were learning life skills. They in turn introduced me to their families. Whenever I travel to Ireland, as I have many times in the past fourteen years, I make it a point to visit these families. I am impressed by their hospitality and friendliness. They have helped me to understand their way of life and the gifts they bring to the country.

Finally, the Church speaks often today of Catholics having a 'preferential option for the poor'. Whatever one's state of life, whatever one's occupation, we are exhorted by Pope John Paul II and others to stand up for the rights of those caught in the vicious cycles of poverty, injustice and violence. Central to this option, in my experience, is making friends with the very people we are defending. This means visiting them in their neighbourhoods, in their homes, and having them as guests in ours. Barriers break down over a meal, alliances are forged in informal situations, friendships are formed when we share, face to face, our dreams and our hopes, our pain and our sorrow. Opportunities for conversion of our hearts to greater compassion may occur, as I have endeavoured to show in this essay.

HOSPICE: A PROPHETIC MOVEMENT

Sheila Cassidy

In 1982 I moved my main professional locus from the cancer wards of Plymouth General Hospital to become the medical director of a small hospice for the dying. My work at the hospital already involved a good deal of terminal care, so when I was offered the job at the hospice I did not see it as a dramatic change of direction. In the years that followed, however, I have become aware that the hospice has come to stand in prophetic relationship to the mainstream of medical care in our area. This role is neither conscious on the part of the hospice nor specifically articulated by anyone, but I believe it is none the less true. Nor are we unique, for throughout the country and in other countries too hospices are having an effect upon medical thought and practice that is quite out of proportion to their size.

They are able to carry out this prophetic function because they fulfil three major criteria: they are drawn from the mainstream of society to live and work at one remove from it; they have the contemplative space to reflect upon the problems confronting them; and they do not choose this role but find themselves speaking a truth that they cannot contain.

In a consideration of the prophetic role of the hospice movement it is important to be clear on the meaning of the word *prophet*, for it is often misused and therefore misunderstood. Prophets are individuals or groups of people who are called both to listen and to speak out. They must listen to God, to the signs of the times, and to the cries of the oppressed, and when they have understood the message, speak out, whatever the personal cost. Prophets are no holier than any one else. They are frequently very wounded people, but, like Jeremiah or Isaiah, they put their woundedness at the service of God. When they hear the voice that says, 'Whom shall I send? Who will be our messenger?' to their horror, they find themselves answering, 'Here I am, send me' (Isaiah 6:8).

Prophetic messages are, almost by definition, unwelcome, because they challenge the accepted status quo. Today's prophets are just as tiresome as the prophets of the Old Testament. Amnesty International shouts its truth about imprisonment and torture from the rooftops and persists in writing importunate letters to busy politicians and dictators. Greenpeace gets its silly rainbow boats in the way of important nuclear tests. And the anti-smoking lobby keeps drawing attention to the huge revenues governments receive from cigarette advertising. It is the same in the medical world. Just when the government is trying to tidy up the shambolic National Health Service and make it more efficient, health workers *will* go on about the emotional needs of the sick and ask for more resources for such tedious and unproductive groups as the elderly, the handicapped and the dying.

The first and most obvious thing for which people seek the help of a hospice is the relief of pain. Everyone is afraid of pain, and well they might be, for it saps the strength and crowds the consciousness until the person is overwhelmed and wishes quite simply for death. Pain is very common (though not inevitable) in advanced cancer, and yet in a hospice setting it nearly always comes rapidly under control. Why? Why is this not the case in hospital, and in the community? Do we have special instruments, techniques that are not available to ordinary people? The answer, absurdly, is no. We use the same drugs, the same techniques and practically no high-tech medicine. It is a question of experience in diagnosis and in the handling of a few very common drugs and of a meticulous attention to detail. More than anything it is an attitude which says pain is soul-destroying and unnecessary and we will not rest until it is relieved. Perhaps, like the prophets of old, we are the spokespersons for the oppressed. We listen to the cries of the people and try to speak out for them. We realise that they want to be treated as normal, responsible people. They want to have their illness explained to them in words that they can understand, and to be consulted about its treatment. They want to retain their dignity as individuals and keep some control over their lives. They want to participate in their care and share in our decision-making. They want us to be honest with them, warm and humble. More than anything, they want us to combine our competence with compassion and, when our hands are empty, to stay our ground and share the frightening darkness with them. More than anything, they need our love.

What makes the hospice different from the hospital is the philosophy of the hospice movement. It is a philosophy based upon the conviction that people, all people, however far gone, are infinitely precious and their treatment must be tailored to their individual needs. The dying are individuals, complex human beings whose needs are legion: physical, intellectual, emotional, spiritual, social. In hospital, we provide high-quality treatment to the tip of the human iceberg: we diagnose disease and try to cure it. We attend to the basic physical needs as well as our resources permit. We are as patient and kind as we are able to be, given the shortage of personnel and the pressures of work. We try to help the families when they are in difficulty, but mostly, we dare not open the Pandora's box of human fear and anguish. We are not encouraged to ask people what it *really* feels like to have cancer, to be dying. We are not taught to hold their hands when they are lonely or afraid, or to cradle them, sobbing, in our arms, smoothing their hair, holding them until the paroxysms pass. We are not trained to *love*. Or rather we are trained to *suppress* our love, to don a protective uniform especially for work, a uniform that keeps us at a safe distance from our patients so that our meetings are those of professional and client, not of the frail human beings that we all are. Could it be that we are unconsciously denying our patients the one thing that they long for, the one gift that it is in our power to give: our human warmth?

The dying are a people on a journey. They are an uprooted people, dispossessed, marginalised, travelling fearfully into the unknown. The conditions and speed of the journey may vary – sometimes the movement is barely perceptible, like the moving floors at an airport, but sometimes the tracks hurtle through the night, throwing their bewildered occupants from side to side with all the terror of the line to Auschwitz. Above all, the dying are alone and they are afraid.

Paradoxically, these fears are rarely articulated, so strong is the cult of the stiff upper lip or the desire to protect those closest to them. What they want more than anything is that this thing should not be happening to them, that it should turn out to be a bad dream, that they should be rescued, cured, kissed better, made whole. But since this cannot be, they want someone to comfort them, to hold their hand, to face the unknown with them. They need a companion, a friend.

Love, especially in the hospice context, can be a very practical and earthly business. I think especially of David, a bachelor in his late forties, a wonderful man, one of the poor of our successful, affluent society who has lost even the one possession that remained to him: his physical integrity. By the time he was referred to our service, the cancer in his mouth had recurred despite treatment and he had a painful malignant ulcer where his teeth should have been. I saw him regularly in my outpatient clinic, always accompanied by a young psychiatric community nurse who cared for him, but he refused to be admitted, jealously guarding his independence despite a growing terror of choking to death. On Christmas Day he gave in and came to spend the day with us. Never will I forget the moment when he handed me a bottle of champagne and a torn scrap of paper on which he scribbled, 'I appreciate all that you're doing for me'. I asked him if he could manage a little liquidised turkey and was hard-pressed not to cry when he said, 'Thank you, but a little watery porridge will be fine.'

It is difficult to explain the love-hate relationships we have with these spectres at the feast of life, gaunt figures with their tissues and their vomit bowls, oblivious to the appalling stench from their foul necrotic tumours. We are not immune to the smell of decaying flesh, and, like anyone, we long to escape to where the air is pure. And yet, cohabiting peacefully with our distaste, is a real love for these broken people. People mutter of people like David, 'How awful! If it were a dog, you'd have it put down.' But then, David is not a dog, but a man with cancer in his mouth, who is living out his last precarious days, loved and cherished in a way that he has never known before. It is in this lavishing of love on patients like David that the hospice movement stands in a prophetic relationship to society at large, for it affirms the value of the brain-damaged, the mutilated and the old to a world which values the clever, the physically beautiful and the athletic.

What I am saying when I talk about love is not an argument for more hospices; I am simply talking about a set of attitudes. It is about developing a degree of insight into the patients' world – what the psychologists call empathy. With that insight goes a heightened sensitivity to the patient's distress and a searching for ways to relieve it – or at least not to make it worse. At heart, professional loving is about competence, empathy and communication. It is about becoming sensitive to the pain of others and therefore becoming terribly vulnerable. For me, as for many, it is a way of caring that I aspire to, but achieve only some of the time.

The spirituality of those who care for the dying must be the spirituality of the companion, of the friend who walks alongside, helping, sharing and sometimes just sitting, empty-handed, when we would rather run away. It is a spirituality of presence, of being alongside, watchful, available; of being there. Put like this, the care of the dying seems an impossibly daunting task. Who but a fool or a saint would deliberately expose themselves, day after day, to intolerable pain and sadness? And yet, of course, people do. Why? Who knows. I suppose the obvious answer is that it is a calling, what in religious jargon is called a vocation. Some people are attracted to this kind of work, they find they have a gift for it and discover that it is enormously rewarding. It is not easy – never that – but somehow what one pays out is given back a hundredfold.

If death is in reality birth into new life, then the carer is one who attends the person in labour, comforting, encouraging, facilitating as new life emerges from the old. Watching people grow in spiritual stature is one of the most exciting aspects of working with the dying – as indeed it is in any ministry. Growth, however, is always the work of the spirit – we cannot make it happen. We can only try to provide an environment in which it can occur, if it is meant to. And occur it does: people who seem quite ordinary gradually transcend their human bonds of fear and self-interest, until their only concern is for others. They become somehow translucent, incandescent, glowing like candles in the dark.

It is my experience that those involved in caring – whether it be for alcoholics, drug addicts, the handicapped, the poor or the otherwise dispossessed – are called to a particular experience of Christ and his kingdom. They are called to share in his ministry of healing, of forgiveness, of the washing of feet, and in doing so they are caught up in the whole drama of redemptive suffering. This involvement can be like meeting a giant wave: it can catch you unawares so that you are bowled over and over, terrified, with your lungs full of water and mouth full of sand. Then after a while, if the ministry is right for you, you learn to cope with the sea. Sometimes you ride the waves, sometimes you duck just in time, diving blindly into the dark water – and sometimes your timing is wrong and you get knocked over again. Then, just as you think, 'I've had it,' you surface, amazed to find that you are still alive.

THE TIME OF THE CLOWN

Joe Lucey

About the call and all that

In terms of personality, I am more tangential than centre-line. I find the centre claustrophobic. I need instinctively to get out. The air is freer, wilder, along the edge. I imagine core instincts such as these to be the bits that have become me and are becoming me, bits of clay that were fired together into a way of being, a way of seeing, a way of understanding. Into that firing there came the kiss of a dream who named herself 'fire'. And somewhere between the firing and the fire, a laugh began to dance, a baby began to cry. I don't know when the call began or where it ends but I imagine it began somewhere in the dreaming of love. And love never ends, the disciple says.

It's dinner-time. Father and nine children sit at table, busily negotiating food, strategy as necessary as salt, courage as necessary as pepper. Fast learning and fast eating becoming core Lucey traits. Mother arrives down with baby number ten. He has been around now for two days, but he's still a novelty to some of the younger ones. Baby looks at his world. Baby listens to the noise. Baby starts to cry. 'Baby is hungry,' they say. (Baby lesson one: I am never fully understood. I am misunderstood. Sometimes I am understood.)

Years later. It's dinner-time. Father, mother and ten children sit at table. It's the day of the pig, three days before the fish, one day after the egg. The children air opinions and breathe rituals. 'I can't get a word in edgeways.' My father's voice lives me. The rituals live me. The way to breathe lives me. The stories told at table after table after table live me. Her silence during so much of the meal lives me. His sharing his spoon lives me. Our common cup, our search for space, our waiting and our finding lives me.

Our warring for more hugs, our battle for more blanket lives me. Am I them, then? The stories that they packed into my genes that night when they sent me off. Odysseus was but a paddle in the sea. Am I them, then? The wood stories that unlocked as I grew up with the trees.

Perhaps this Jesus is the breath of me, but I still don't know him. I still do battle with the breath. I am still suspicious of the fire's kiss. And yet the blessing abounds. At every turn, at every corner, and most of all in the goodness and friendship of young people along the edge, the blessing is there, upholding.

Streetdiary: Friday 20th

Tonight on streetwork, I met a young woman who had been sleeping rough for almost three years. None of the homeless hostels could cope with her outbursts. Any attempt to hold her had failed. While in prison she had frequently attempted suicide. Tonight she sat quietly on the steps of one of the bigger stores. 'Hello Patricia,' I said. 'How are you tonight?'

Patricia didn't reply. She sat there silently, refusing even to look up and acknowledge my presence. I decided to sit with her on the steps and to listen for a while to her silence. Her silence filled the street with pain. It screamed at the emptiness of the haunting shadows. In her silence she had invited me to listen to her story, which that night could find no words. Her silence reminded me again of the depths in which we walk, of the vast experiences which we carry, and of how little of each other we really get to know.

At times I fantasise about accompaniment. I imagine ministry as a way of being with another, and yet I can be blind to the other's signals and deaf to the other's cry. Our language fails us. I wish to make contact through word, through touch, and I fail. I am left with the spaces of non-communication, the mystery spaces. In the end I don't know if I have ever met the other, except perhaps in the dreamscape of fools, whose desire to meet is the perfection of their meeting.

That space we share when we meet each other is a space of mystery, of knowing and of not knowing, of trust and doubt. In so far as my ministry is a ministry of accompaniment, it is a ministry that refuses to allow the illusion of success. My walking with you is a humble path, a path where I can never be certain which turn to take, where each step moves us both into the mystery of the one who calls. In this space between us, we'll talk of the glimpses we get, of the joys and fears, of the news and the climate of the day. In the evening we'll gather around a fire so that the dream in my heart and the dream in your heart may find a voice and echo in the melodies of our song.

To accompany you on your journey, I need to inhabit my own journey and face again the poverty of my heart. At times, I too doubt the story of the dream, I too suspect that the pilgrimage is a farce, the idle tale of a jaded wizard. At times, I too am drawn to the addictions that are strewn across our way. I yearn for satisfaction, for comfort, for contentment, for anything that will fill the void I sometimes feel within. I long for anything that dulls the pain and deludes me into thinking that I am part of an exciting plot and that I am important, essential to the unfolding theme.

I am a poor man who meets you on your journey, not so much a knowledgeable guide but a beggar who forages some scraps for an evening feast. I am a poor man whose only wealth is in my dreams and in the stories I tell, stories to warm a night and speed a way to dawn. At times some travellers pass who have no time to wait. A village fair is calling them, the hour is near, so much will happen for them there. This little patch of road is boring them. Their pace quickens to a merchant's pace. The busyness is all.

I am a poor man who meets with other poor ones along a little backward way.

Song of the fool

I come to you, poor fool that I am,
carrying in my arms fragile tokens of my love.
Away from you, the ache of my aloneness
groans and pines for a different way.
My dream of you embalms the soreness of my primal scar
and lullabies the tears until the spices
blend to the scents of dawn.
Away from you I dream of meeting you.
I strategy each step, and weave these love-tokens
from the bits of wood and straw and golden thread
I find along my wanderer's way.

What might I do in meeting you, poor fool that I am?
I might bedew your path with petals of wild flowers,
and kiss your body, beautiful in its boundedness,
and whisper love-tales into your skin,
so that somewhere within,
two flames of love might burn as one.

What then? What might the burning birth?
Poor fools might birth a dance,
and in the newness of their movement
sketch forth the patterning of a different way,
perhaps even to choreograph an eight-day festival,
to the god beyond gods,
to the fire beyond flames,
to the love in whom all love
captures union in the differentiation of being.

Poor fools. We meet in wonderland
and dance new rituals along the thresholds of mystery
ebbing and flowing with the serenity and the passion of a life.

I've got an address!

David arrived at the centre grinning broadly. 'I've got an address!' he said, his eyes twinkling with a mixture of relief and devilment – relief because he could now get money from the Welfare; devilment because the address was not his own. 'Paddy is letting me use his address,' he explained. 'The Welfare will never find out.'

On National Census night I was asked to list the names of the people I met who were of no fixed abode, who were not sleeping 'under any roof'. That is the nearest a homeless person comes to legal recognition. In Ireland, one cannot be registered for voting purposes, or in order to receive State assistance, or even to sign on the 'live register' of the unemployed, without an address. If you have no address, you are, as far as the State is concerned, as good as dead.

In a sense, my address sets a boundary to the place from which I describe myself. When I share an address with another, we share a world of agreed limits. It can be a prison cell or a mansion but within that world we are contracted together on a basis of trust and common understanding. I can be described by my address. When people know my address, they know where to find me. Addresses offer us points of reference, they help to keep us connected, they map the geography of our conversations.

It can be very threatening when I meet someone who has no address, someone who is of no fixed abode. This 'vagrant' reminds me that my own address may not even be desirable. If others move about between addresses, perhaps I can also. Perhaps I too can question the limits I have set to my world, and change the location from which I describe myself.

But it takes a great effort to break from the gravity pull of my home world in order to explore other worlds. It takes great energy to break from the comfort of my rooted place, even if my rooted place is choked with weeds, and to dare to be elsewhere. And there is a great risk in moving. I too might be labelled bad or mad.

But if I do what is expected of me and if I settle down, do the limits of my address not live me? Do I not become blind to the alternatives and swallow each gulp of local air as if the local is the only truth and the universe is all a lie?

And if I do not move out from my address, if only for a while, how can I ever meet you? I will sit all day and all night longing for you to visit me and you will sit all day and all night longing for me to visit you, both imprisoned by the terror that if we move out from our addresses, we will be no more. Perhaps if we live in neighbouring addresses, we can lean through the top floor windows and stretch our arms and hands until the fingers meet and that touch will perhaps heal the aloneness of our solitary places.

When David arrived in the centre today, grinning broadly, is it any wonder he had a twinkle in his eye?

Streetdiary: Monday 30th

The amusement arcade was dark and smoky. Heavy rock blared from the speakers, interrupted only by the beat of the video games and gambling machines. There was something addictive in the air. A group of young people were smoking dope in one corner. Others sat huddled around a new machine. Arcades are a popular haunt for those who are out of home. There you find shelter and music and company. It's easy to hide there and to forget the pain and loneliness of the streets, even for a while.

There must have been fifty young people hanging around there today. Now and then, an older man came in, played on one of the machines and then left, followed by one of the younger boys. Today I was very conscious of being a priest in that place, claiming that seedy cavern as my sanctuary and recognising the pool table as my altar, the place on which to offer the sacrifices and pain of a broken humanity. And the place to claim that there is light, even in the midst of the darkness, and to claim that love has conquered even death.

Streetdiary: Thursday 2nd
On the streets, groups of young people are constantly forming, breaking up, re-forming: the ebb and flow of the street tides, an odyssey of attachment, a quest for home. Through membership of my group, I inhabit a meaningful conversation. Boundaries are set by the themes we choose which define for us what is normal and what is unacceptable. Sometimes we dress our story in colours and clothes and hair-styles that are loud and daring. We are companions around a night fire. We belong together because for us there is truth in the lie that none of us is wanted. We're different from 'normal' people so we create a normality of our difference. As those banished from the tribe, we create our own nomadic culture. We live the stories of the here and now, localised to our street corner, distinguished by the territory over which we reign. Moment by moment, the flow of time carries us along, presenting new excitements and new tragedies. Rachel has been arrested. Domo has been beaten up. And in the hidden place between us, love stories are sometimes told and silent screams are sometimes heard.

The Frontier
The land of homelessness is at or beyond the Frontier. From one perspective, the Frontier is a threshold of banishment. It is the place of the curse. Those who are sent there carry with them the masks that others have made for them to wear. They are the masks of monsters and fools, of madmen and murderers. Theirs is the history where story after story unfolded themes of rejection punctuated by despair.

'How much more do I have to take?' asks Jimmy as he shows me his recent scars. He tells me of the relief he feels when he is cutting himself, how the flow of blood seems to ease the tension, how the sting of wounded flesh relieves the agony of an inner world, a world confused by the lie and rebelling because somewhere within there is still a part of faith in another truth.

All Jimmy knows about himself is what others have told him.

He knows himself as the one who was known as a child to be dirt, as the one who was known to be unwanted. He knows himself as the one who became known later by what he did, by the ways he broke the law, by the number of charges he had, by the length of his criminal record. In prison, he became known by the offences he had committed and by the length of his sentence. And all the time he knew himself as the one who was known by others. And all the time he remained unknown. And all the time something else within screamed against the loneliness of not being personally known.

I am condemned to these masks. I am told I'm ugly. And yet I am afraid of what I might be like if I remove my ugliness, I'm afraid of what might happen if I mould a different way of being. I am storied to these limits, to this cursed place, where the only meaning I can give is the meaning that my tribe has given me. To survive out here, I play by different rules. I am an untouchable. My caste is fixed. I have never known another way.

From another perspective, however, the Frontier can also be a land of possibility. From the Frontier, I can see the system in a another way. The Frontier can be a place of blessing. It can also be a threshold of hope. By listening to the stories of those whom the story of the culture rejects, I can glimpse the underlying meaning and limitedness of the culture. When I move away from the centre and dare to live at the edge, I find myself living at a place where the system is not neat and tidy any more, but it is crumbling and even becoming meaningless. When I live at the edge, the chaos of the outside begins to have as large an effect on me as the security of the centre. When I face the fears of the Frontier world, when I realise that the story by which I have lived my life is not the only story, when I glance beneath the system and see how wobbly the foundations are, when I count the cracks that are appearing, when I dare to imagine that the centre may not hold, then perhaps the universe can begin again. On this Frontier, everything is always in the throes of birth. It is the kingdom of midwifery and nurseries. Yesterday's alternatives have crumbled. Only the new remains.

In this place of threshold blessings, two people can risk encountering each other, perhaps for the first time. The land of homelessness is a threshold land, a land of banishment and hope, a land of curses and blessings.

Streetdiary: Monday 27th

Along the quays, we came upon a few familiar faces. One of them was Jim. He is about seventeen. There are several who hang around the quays late at night. Sometimes, they disappear off the scene and we don't meet again for weeks. Our chat began. Soon three other fellows joined us. They seemed to be drawn out of the dark corners. It is as if they were telling us that we were safe, that talking with us would not bring them any harm, that we were not going to judge them or moralise with them. We had a couple of laughs. Derek indicated that he had some personal stuff to sort out. He agreed to come into the centre the next day for a chat. After about half an hour, our little group broke up, each taking up a different position along the pavement. As we left, a car approached, slowed down and parked near by.

There was a sadness and confusion in my heart as we walked away, leaving those young people on the street to ply their trade, their prices fixed, a confidence in their custom, yet always fearful of being beaten or raped. The more I reflected, the more I began to rage at the horror of their reality, the brutality of the suffering and abuse. And again I wondered about God. Things seem to have changed very little since Jesus' day.

Woman without price

I thought I was cheap. Sometimes I played with prices but in my heart I knew my business fee bore no relation to the cheapness of my life. I knew people used to sneer at me, commenting on me as I passed, raping me with their eyes, belittling me with their tongues. 'Can't you even take a joke?' the men would snap, if ever I glared at their hypocrisy. And the village women could find no words to capture their disgust. They'd call to their children if I approached on the street. They'd look away if I bid them the blessing of the day. Their silence towards me was worse than if they had called me 'whore'.

I often tried to pretend not to notice, pretending to be unaffected by their shaming. But from my outcast place, each day and night groaned beneath the burden of my pain. I was almost relieved when the priests told me I would die. And in a way, that day I did die.

'You're free,' he said. At first I thought again of how men priced my life, battling with me over the pennies of my sweat. 'You're free,' he said again, as if his commerce was sketched from a different view. Only in time did I come to see myself a little more by his eyes, to know myself a little more as he knows me, to understand that I am not alone and that I am of such value, I am free.

Streetdiary: Saturday 8th

It was one of those invitations I couldn't refuse. Willie and Seamus had decided to leave Dublin. They were now in their late teens and after nine months on the streets, they had had enough. Now that summer was approaching, Galway presented a better alternative. They had asked me around to their squat so that we could have a going-away party before they left. They would meet me at the corner of Leeson Street. The time was fixed. I was to bring my guitar.

The night in question turned out to be extremely wet. As soon as I arrived at the meeting place, our little group took off down one of the side streets. The only way into the squat was through the back of the house, up the fire-escape and in a second-floor window that had been left open. To get to the fire-escape, we had to climb two or three walls and dodge through the briars and weeds of a large overgrown garden. Such acrobatics weren't really my scene. I was drenched to the skin. I worried about damaging my guitar. I wondered at the madness of what I had let myself in for.

Needless to say, I had dropped to the end of the little

squadron. My thoughts were busy with manoeuvres and with trying to plan the easiest return route for whenever I would head home. I didn't expect Willie to wait behind for me at the foot of the fire-escape. Nor did I expect what he then said to me: 'You really have to go out of your way to get to your little parish, don't you?'

When we finally got to the room at the top of the house, the candles were already lighting. Teresa and Linda had arranged the blankets in a circle and they were waiting for us to arrive. There was a packet of biscuits there and some fresh water in a can. The folks had gathered. It was time to tell the stories, sing the songs and in the sharing, edge our way to dawn.

Later, Willie's comment haunted me, his knowing we were Church, his identifying us as a parish on the edge. Through Willie and his friends, I began to hear again a call to walk the wastelands amongst those who do not belong, to hang around the scrublands amongst those banished from the tribe. Our gathering in the squat reminded me too of how much my pain also pines for rituals of healing, of how my wounds also ache for recognition and yearn to be included in the human dream.

I was reminded of how so much of western society seems starved of ritual and threshold stories. Our rites of passage have been discarded and we are left confused about the tasks of our age and the meaning of our journeys. Finding ourselves unable to journey on, we live in fear of being gobbled up by the threshold guardian or of being banished to that threshold world, inhabited only by the lost. Young homeless people reminded me that night of society's failed rituals, of society's lack of interest in the greatness of the least, of casualness regarding our direction and of confusion about who we really are.

Somewhere East of Eden

It was still dark when I met the homeless one.

Who are you? he asked.

I replied

I am a homeless one, a wanderer abroad who forages his way
    through time,

seeking the touch of strangers,

seeking to kiss and to be kissed into that union

which dulls the memory of that umbilical nightmare

that cut me off for ever.

I am the son of Adam, the son of Eve.

I am the carrier of their scar,

the deep suspicion that drove them running out of Eden,

nourished by the fruit of knowledge,

but plagued by the confusion of truth.

Adam, Eve, rejected ones, banished ones

for ever to mistrust a promise made

for ever to suspect the gift of covenant.

Bonds break. Why risk the pain?

I am a homeless one, befriending places that are dark,

meandering through the streets,

not knowing if I'm searching or hiding,

fearful that if I rest in one place I might understand that I am
    alone.

I am the unsure one,

who traces cracks across the belly of every sure thing.

I am a restless vagabond who roams from world to world,

cohabiting only for a while.

I sleep in snatches.

And when I sleep, I always dream of home.

Streetdiary: no date

There is so much suffering in these incessant nights of humanity,
the suffering of the one who is abandoned, who lives totally
alone, cut off from all meaningful relationships, believing only in

the lie of rejection, the creed of despair. The suffering seems to come from new depths all the time. There seems to be no part of the human spirit that is not torn by the pain of suffering, leaving in its trail the primeval ache, the groaning, the cry. Each day, new scars come out of hiding. Each night, new stories unfold. Themes overlap. Themes of wounded sexuality, confused desires, the vulnerable seeking love, the powerful seeking to use, a litany of inadequate encounters. In place of communion, there are damaged capacities for relationship. Autistic barriers mock at intimacy. Dangerous attractions are driven underground, only to surge again in the wastelands of the night.

Somewhere on the other side of Emmaus
Wandering a longing boreen,
seeking hedgy shelters and draining sleep.
Drifting through the city, meandering the back streets
with the same rural restlessness.
I must get food.
I beg but no one notices how poor I am.
They see me as useful, talented,
but not poor, not hungry.

Turning a corner we meet one day.
It could have been by accident.
And when I looked into your eyes,
I saw that you could see me,
as clearly as I could see you.
I did not know your name.
I did not know my own name.
But I knew you were my brother, my sister,
You too were hungry,
You too were poor.

When we embraced then,
the beauty of your touch caressed my emptiness,

and the strength of your arms surprised away
my sense of shame.
And when you took from your overcoat a crust of bread,
and when you broke it with me,
your eyes sparkled and I laughed too,
knowing that the companion's feast,
this beggar's dream,
whirled us up into the beauty and the dance of God.

Thank you, beggar, for dancing with me.
and for dreaming even in the poorest parts of my being.

Streetdiary: Wednesday 29th

We had a lot of trouble in the centre tonight. Two of the young men got into a bad fight. Some cups were broken, and for a few moments, things seemed to get out of control. It's always a struggle to keep the boundaries safe and to ensure that the place is secure. Some of the youngsters seem to cry out at times for someone to control them. Often their cry is like that of a baby who just wants to be held. In a way so much of the acting-out behaviour is a cry for that order, a cry for help to clarify the limits and boundaries of one's world, a cry for the security that only an embrace can give. It is as if the youngster is crying, 'Please hold me up, for everything around me is falling apart.'

So much of the work in the centre is around creating a safe place, a place to relax without threat, a place to disclose without fear, to cry without being smothered, to be at peace without having to hide the wounds.

There seems to be a deep connection between the aggressiveness of acting out and the cry for safety and order. It is almost as if I cannot be gentle unless I am sure of the boundaries of my world. When I know my personal limits, the space between us will be a gentle space. Gentleness invites me to be confident and not afraid to wander out towards the other.

Streetdiary: no date

Waiting around. Waiting for the welfare officer. Waiting in the dinner queue. Waiting for the soup run. Waiting the night away. People who are poor, who know themselves as needy, seem to have a rich capacity for waiting. Often when I sit with them, I learn to wait too. I learn to listen to the ways my busyness cloaks me from the nakedness of my own needs. I learn to listen in a new way to the Gospel stories of waiting, bridesmaids and servants, waiting through the night with flasks filled with the wisdom of their longing.

Song of the servant

For days and days I have been awaiting your return.
The village folk all mock me as they pass. They say,
'You foolish one. Why do you wait for him?
The banquet has been cancelled. The bridegroom will not
    come.'
And yet I wait for you.
'Perhaps he'll come at dawn,' I say to those who jeer.
'Perhaps at dawn he'll cross the hill,
beautiful in the radiance of the sun,
his hair moistened by the morning dew.'
And still I wait for you.

In the darkness of the nights,
the wildness of my fears invades my fantasy,
tormenting me lest you be wounded or slain.
But then I hear your voice again:
'Trust me. I will come.
Wait for me at the foot of the hill,
and you will walk me to my bride.'

I never knew a servant's life could be like this,
or that a servant's love could pain so deep,
for as each hour of waiting comes and goes,

my love for you aches deeper than an ocean cave,
my longing rolls across the desert plain
and screams the heavens, pining just one drop
of rain, to soothe and care
the emptiness of my heart.

Your servant will wait for you, fair Lord,
and in my watching, sing of how
in truth and wonder I am blessed,
for the deep poverty of my longing
is but a testament to the richness
of my love for you.

Streetdiary: Monday 12th

When we met the 'hoods gang' this evening, they were in a very bouncy mood. They had made a friend of a security man in one of the cafés and so were guaranteed entry. There was a music video there and they wanted us to go with them, not so that we could buy them food, but so that they could give us music and fun. We went to the café. All were admitted except the dog. We found a corner of our own. The music was chosen. There was dancing and lots of fun. Street kids don't want martyrs to wail for them. They want friends with whom they can laugh and dance and sing. I thought of the stories of another age when dungeon laughter mocked the prison guards, when dancers reigned from the midst of the fire, when songs of freedom broke the slavery of the night.

Streetdiary: Wednesday 14th

Gerry told me his story today of how he had been working for the past six months with a circus. The circus offered only seasonal work and so for the winter Gerry returned to the city, hoping to get a bed in one of the homeless hostels.

In the circus, Gerry was like a herald. He was one of those who travelled three days ahead of the circus, putting up the posters in the towns and villages, which the circus was to visit. His job was to tell people that the circus was coming, that they were to prepare a space and be ready to celebrate. He was like Man Friday, announcing the Sunday feast.

It often surprises me when I see the clown peeping out at me around the corners of streets. Somehow I don't expect to meet a clown in such a shadowy place. And yet the clown's home is the threshold place, the world between worlds, always edging his way to new possibilities, listening to the songs of the present but already preparing a melody for the future. The clown remains an outsider. She observes from the sidelines, tracing newness along the frontier. Through play, the clown pre-empts the possibility of a future which can be different from the past. Standing at the limit of a world where meaning is not fixed but where choices are plentiful, the clown says that there can be another way. The present is not so much determined by the past, but through anticipation is defined by the future.

The threshold place of homelessness invites an exploration, not only of the tragic depths of human suffering, but also of the evolving possibilities of alternative ways of being.

The time of the clown

1

It was the middle of winter when the circus came to our village.
Buntings threw themselves on lamp-posts
    and held hands as they laughed their way around the square.
There was a smell of something sacred in the air.
The colours crossed themselves,
    sensing a call to dance a rainbow
    arching an entrance to the sanctuary.

The children were content to wait in little groups,
    singing time away.
They had seen the signs, the promises of joy.
And they remembered the stories which the old

181

    people told them
as they kept company with the winter fires,
stories of how the hedge would kiss the tree,
and the wolf would mother the child.
And they remembered the old songs,
    'When the Carnival comes midwinter
we will be hounded into spring.
The frost and ice will be warmed away,
with the passion of a lover.'

At noon, the burst of children's laughter called
    the village out to dance.
Each warp and limp of rustic life came out of hiding.
All knew the hour had come.
This was the time of the clown.
This was the day of the festival.

When the clown appeared he stood at the rainbow arch
    and winked at the colours overhead.
He too was dressed for the sun.
He too glided on the wind.
Children danced on the palm of his hand.
His sleeves were wide with laughter.
Each gesture beckoned a smile.
Head chasing heels, giggled volcanoes
    of nonsense and joy.

2
It was at sunset he came to me,
    a tired clown, weary with the day.
'Come aside,' I said, 'and rest a while,
    for the night is about to fall,
    and alone, in darkness, I am afraid.'

He sat with me, this tired clown,
and in the whispers of midwinter night he said,
   'You will never be alone again.
   Each night is but the seed of day.
   Each darkness but a birthpang of light.
   It's when I'm tired I bring most joy.'

3
Months passed.
Some villagers died, some were born.
Spring rolled over on the grass and as their game went on,
   summer crept into position.
Midsummer festival exploded into the night.
The wind whistled the trees. Bonfires blazed.
The children sat near by, fascinated by the dancing shadows.
(No one had ever told them that shadows could be fun.)
And the grown-ups seemed drunk with new wine.

A little one whispered,
   'Can you see the signs everywhere? He must have returned.'
Yes, I had seen them.
It was like recognising a favourite overture,
   a melody packed with promise.
He was here all right. His scent filled the air.
In each laugh, I could hear his laughter.
The clown had returned.

Just before dawn he came to me, a tired clown,
   weary from a night of fun.
'Come with me,' he said, 'to a quiet place,
   for the morning will soon sing to us
   and together we can welcome its praise.'
As we rested, waiting for the sun to tiptoe through the night,
   I asked my companion
   for the secret of his clowning.

'Let go,' he said.

'Laughter and dance are the children of abandonment.
Joy and grief blossom from the one shoot.
Let the little ones teach you.
They know my secret.
Wherever I hide, they find me.
Whatever my guise, they welcome me home.
To be a clown means to live with the little ones.
Love's laughter mingles with their tears.
And in their dance, the dawn etches a new day.'

Streetdiary: Friday 24th

'Any chance of few candles, Joe? The churches are all locked and it's pitch black in the squat. You couldn't even see Redser trying to rob your smokes. But then, he's so clumsy you'd catch him anyway.'

With that, Redser gave Jimmy a thump and ran off. Before running after him, Jimmy said: 'We'll wait for you at the Corner Shop. Come up anyway, even if you can't get the candles.'

I managed to get a few candles and soon the little group of us was dodging our way from back street to back lane until we reached the spot, derelict and unsuspected yet, a great find. When we got in I lit one of the candles. There was a vague movement from the far corner where about five more bodies were huddled together under a few old blankets.

There was something bothering Jimmy. All of a sudden he said to me: 'Joe, give us a blessing, will you?'

I became uncomfortable. I wasn't really prepared for this. I immediately got suspicious and wondered what Jimmy was up to.

'Are you serious, Jim?' I asked.

'Of course I'm serious. You're a priest aren't you? I need your blessing.'

I leaned over, touched his head, and quietly prayed a blessing on Jimmy. Soon after, Redser spoke up: 'Joe, I want a blessing too.'

Then Gerry from across the room shouted: 'I want a blessing too.'

And soon blessings became the order of the night. 'Bless the squat, Joe, that it won't burn down and that the cops won't find us.'

In a few minutes, the squat was a buzz of excitement. By now all the candles were lighting and a warm glow danced with the shadows on the wall. Then Jimmy turned to me again: 'Isn't it great, Joe? Isn't it great to blessed? Isn't it great to think that you're okay, that you're loved? It's brilliant.' And with that he jumped onto the mattress and he laughed long and loud, like a little child who was being tickled by his father.

I stayed there for a while and we swapped some stories of life on the streets. As I went home later that night, I thought of how these youngsters constantly surprise me with their teachings on the meaning of encounter, of what happens between people who allow themselves to be known. They were telling me about my priesthood, about my work as a therapist, about my life. In some ways they were telling me that night that my life might be about blessings, about coaxing away the curse of rejection and in its place proclaiming the embrace of the dawn, the dance of the daughter, the song of the son. They were inviting me to celebrate the light as it gently awakens dark and sleepy corners, and to find in the scarred faces of the little ones, the laughter and the sparkle of one I claim as God.

Streetdiary: no date
It is the utter holiness of this place,
this space of bare feet which only naked touch can serve.
This is the ground on which we stand.
We, the poorest ones who are blessed to hang around
with wounded ones who are considered poor,
those who are in truth our priests, our ministers,
testifying that in their midst there lives

a gift, a love, a holiness
that smiles and cries and screams and sings.

'We will pitch here four tents, Lord.
One for you, one for Domo, one for Redser and one for Rachel.'

This is the sacred shrine, where we enact new rituals
to a crazed and senseless God,
who has lost herself forever in the shawls of the poor,
in the wounds of the outcast,
in the gasps and pants of the one who doesn't want to die.
This is the holy cloister, where we dance to a stooping God,
who has dust on his feet and dust in her hair,
the nomad who dances the desert,
keeping company with those journeying into freedom.
This is the inner sanctuary,
where we sing to a God who sings the sun
but is still cold when we are cold,
a God who became flesh and pitched tent
amongst Domo and Redser and Rachel and me.

Streetdiary: Wednesday 24th
For some reason, I thought a lot about Don Bosco today, and of his pilgrimage with the poorer ones of Turin. And I wondered, after he died, what happened to his shoes? I suspect the dirt from the streets was washed off and that the shoes were polished up like new, and put in a glass case.

And I was thinking too of the pilgrims of that faraway time, the starry-eyed who travelled from the east. And I thought of how it was the night pilgrims and the night shepherds who were the ones to find the child hidden away amongst the poor. And I sensed a glory tucked away amidst the etchings of the night.

Towards dawn
Domo and Redser, Rachel and me, what is that space we share?

What is the landscape between us like, that territory of encounter? At times perhaps it's like an earthquake zone, a classified disaster where we wander amongst the rubble of our lives, reclaiming parts that are lost and frightened, parts that are afraid to move lest the ground on which we walk should cave in again. At times the territory between is rugged and mountainous. At times it's free-flowing and open, like a canal tripping through the midlands or the lowlands. It is the landscape for experimentation and adventure.

I am very threatened by adventure. Although I dream of being a knight, the windmills of my day frighten me back to sleep. New visions disturb me. They invite me to the possibility of change and, although I have made a profession of change, I'm terrified of it. I'm terrified to leave home, to leave the familiar place of my childhood dreams, the place of my parents and my foreparents and to become poor again and to wander again in the desert of my powerlessness and insecurity. I cling to my family gods, my treasured inheritance, my guarantee of protection from the storms of life, my recipe for wisdom in the face of trials. I dare not leave these gods behind, and yet I know I must if I am to become myself.

I have walked some places where some homeless people walk. I have listened to their stories. Their stories coax me to be confident. They encourage me to string and lute new melodies from the frightened spaces within. They invite me to sit with them through the night, beggar to beggar, around the desert fires, learning to be a lover rather than a master, learning to celebrate the touch, gentle in its respectfulness, seeking not to dominate but to share. Through that night, which stories threshold kingdoms, we may come to recognise ourselves, perhaps for the first time, and once again trace pointers to a new home. The night passes, sometimes very slowly, sometimes with terror and much pain. Perhaps our stories help us pass the night, dreaming us to another place, a place perhaps where we will learn to dance again in the arms of a new dawn.

THE CONTRIBUTORS

Sheila Cassidy is a Catholic laywoman. A medical doctor, she specialises in the treatment and care of people with cancer, especially those in the final stages of the illness. She has been closely involved with the hospice movement. She has published several books, including *Light from the Dark Valley* (1994, Darton, Longman & Todd).

Edward J. Farrell is a priest who worked in a poor parish in inner-city Detroit. He gives talks and retreats worldwide. He has published many books, including *Free to be Nothing* (1989, Dominican Publications).

Edwina Gateley, a Catholic lay missionary who works with prostitutes, has written extensively and gives talks worldwide about her work. *I Hear a Seed Growing* (1990, Source Books) is an account of her life and work.

John Halsey is an Anglican priest who lives as part of a small inter-city community near Edinburgh in Scotland, which is devoted to prayer and welcoming the homeless poor.

Tim Kearney is a Catholic layman who has worked for many years in the L'Arche community in France. He now lives and works in the l'Arche community in Cork and is national co-ordinator of l'Arche in Ireland.

Stanislaus Kennedy is a Religious Sister of Charity. Founder and president of Focus Point Ireland, a national organisation which provides a wide range of innovative responses to help homeless people to find and keep home, she has devoted her life to working and campaigning with and for poor. Her publications include *But Where Can I Go?* (1985, available from Focus Point Ireland).

Joe Lucey is a Salesian priest who has worked on the streets with young people out-of-home in inner-city Dublin. He is now director of a drug treatment centre for young people in Dublin.

Bernadette MacMahon is a Daughter of Charity. Trained as a teacher, she has worked with children with reading difficulties and people with mental handicaps. Formerly provincial of her order in Ireland, she now devotes most of her time to the Vincentian Partnership for Justice in Dublin, which works for social change.

Peter McVerry is a Jesuit who is well-known in Ireland for his work with homeless boys and young men and for his tireless campaigning and advocacy on their behalf. He writes and lectures extensively.

Dara Molloy was formerly a Catholic priest. He now lives and works in a small monastic community on Inismór, in the Aran Islands off the Galway coast, where he welcomes people who are in need of rest in a spiritual environment. He is particularly interested in Celtic spirituality.

The late **Henri Nouwen** was a priest and was known worldwide and highly revered as a lecturer (in Harvard and Yale) and writer. In latter years, he devoted his life to living and working in the L'Arche community of Daybreak in Canada. He published several books in his lifetime, including *The Road to Daybreak* (1988, Darton, Longman & Todd), an account of his spiritual journey from the academic world to living and working with people with handicaps.

Max Oliva is a Jesuit who has lived with marginalised people in the United States and many other parts of the world. He has published many books, including *Praying the Beatitudes* (1990, Veritas) and *Free to Pray, Free to Love* (1994, Veritas).

Jean Vanier, a Catholic layman, is the founder of the L'Arche community for people with mental handicaps, which started in France and now has over a hundred communities worldwide. He is one of today's leading spiritual writers, lecturers and retreat leaders and is author of many books, including *Our Journey Home* (1997, Hodder & Stoughton).

* * *

The artist **William Crozier** studied at Glasgow School of Art and has lived and worked in Dublin, Paris, Malaga and London. He exhibits in London, Europe and America, and his work is to be found in many national collections as well as in commercial galleries and in private collections. He says that 'the crossroads of the painting is in a wooded bogland near Ballydehob in West Cork, Ireland. It is a quiet and solemn place and, in over a decade, I have never seen another person coming or going in any direction on these roads. It is impossible not to be aware of the symbolism these roads present; impossible not to feel some disquiet, isolation, a sense of unspecified tragedy that even the beauty of the bog-cotton in the ditch cannot dispel.'